FREMDSPRACHENTEXTE

Arthur Miller

n

ns

m

Herausgegeben von
Manfred und Gunda Pütz

Philipp Reclam jun. Stuttgart

Diese Ausgabe darf nur in der Bundesrepublik Deutschland, in Österreich und in der Schweiz vertrieben werden.

Universal-Bibliothek Nr. 9172
Alle Rechte vorbehalten
© für diese Ausgabe 1984 Philipp Reclam jun. GmbH & Co., Stuttgart
© für den Text 1949 Arthur Miller. Abdruck mit Genehmigung
von International Creative Management, New York
Umschlagabbildung: Erich Ponto in der Aufführung der
Münchener Kammerspiele (1949)
Bibliographisch ergänzte Ausgabe 2002
Gesamtherstellung: Reclam, Ditzingen. Printed in Germany 2003
RECLAM und UNIVERSAL-BIBLIOTHEK sind eingetragene Marken
der Philipp Reclam jun. GmbH & Co., Stuttgart
ISBN 3-15-009172-1

www.reclam.de

Death of a Salesman

The Characters

WILLY LOMAN
LINDA
BIFF
5 HAPPY
BERNARD
THE WOMAN
CHARLEY
UNCLE BEN
10 HOWARD WAGNER
JENNY
STANLEY
MISS FORSYTHE
LETTA

15 *The action takes place in Willy Loman's house and yard
and in various places he visits in the New York and
Boston of today.*

Act One

*A melody is heard, played upon a flute. It is small and
fine, telling of grass and trees and the horizon. The
curtain rises.*

*Before us is the Salesman's house. We are aware of
towering, angular shapes behind it, surrounding it on all
sides. Only the blue light of the sky falls upon the house
and forestage; the surrounding area shows an angry glow
of orange. As more light appears, we see a solid vault of
apartment houses around the small, fragile-seeming
home. An air of the dream clings to the place, a dream
rising out of reality. The kitchen at center seems actual
enough, for there is a kitchen table with three chairs, and
a refrigerator. But no other fixtures are seen. At the back
of the kitchen there is a draped entrance, which leads to
the living-room. To the right of the kitchen, on a level*

[Titelseite (Untertitel):] **requiem:** Totengottesdienst.
6 **towering:** hoch aufragend.
   angular: eckig; kantig.
8 **forestage:** Proszenium; Vorderbühne.
   area: Gebiet, Bereich.
9 **solid:** massiv.
   vault: Gewölbe; hier: Überwölbung.
10 **fragile:** zerbrechlich.
11 **an air of the dream:** ein Hauch von Traum.
   to cling: anhaften.
12 **actual:** wirklich (Gegensatz zu Traum).
14 **fixtures:** Einrichtungsgegenstände.
15 **draped entrance:** Durchgang mit Vorhang.
16 **level:** Ebene; hier: Podest.

*raised two feet, is a bedroom furnished only with a brass
bedstead and a straight chair. On a shelf over the bed a
silver athletic trophy stands. A window opens onto the
apartment house at the side.*
5 *Behind the kitchen, on a level raised six and a half feet, is
the boys' bedroom, at present barely visible. Two beds
are dimly seen, and at the back of the room a dormer
window. (This bedroom is above the unseen living-
room.) At the left a stairway curves up to it from the*
10 *kitchen.*
*The entire setting is wholly or, in some places, partially
transparent. The roof-line of the house is one-dimen-
sional; under and over it we see the apartment buildings.
Before the house lies an apron, curving beyond the*
15 *forestage into the orchestra. This forward area serves as
the back yard as well as the locale of all Willy's imaginings and of his city scenes. Whenever the action is in the
present the actors observe the imaginary wall-lines, entering the house only through its door at the left. But in the*
20 *scenes of the past these boundaries are broken, and
characters enter or leave a room by stepping "through" a
wall onto the forestage.*

---

1 f. **brass bedstead:** Messingbett.
2 **straight:** hier: einfach.
3 **trophy:** Trophäe.
7 **dimly** (adv.): im Dunkel; verschwommen.
7 f. **dormer window** (arch.): Giebel-, Dachbodenfenster.
14 **apron:** Vorfeld.
15 **orchestra:** hier: Orchestergraben.
16 **back yard** (AE): Garten hinterm Haus.
   locale (AE): Schauplatz.
16 f. **imaginings:** (Phantasie-)Vorstellungen.
18 **to observe:** beachten.
   imaginary: nur in der Einbildung bestehend.

From the right, Willy Loman, the Salesman, enters,
carrying two large sample cases. The flute plays on. He
hears but is not aware of it. He is past sixty years of age,
dressed quietly. Even as he crosses the stage to the
5 *doorway of the house, his exhaustion is apparent. He*
unlocks the door, comes into the kitchen, and thankfully
lets his burden down, feeling the soreness of his palms. A
word-sigh escapes his lips – it might be "Oh, boy, oh,
boy." He closes the door, then carries his cases out into
10 *the living-room, through the draped kitchen doorway.*
Linda, his wife, has stirred in her bed at the right. She
gets out and puts on a robe, listening. Most often jovial,
she has developed an iron repression of her exceptions to
Willy's behavior – she more than loves him, she admires
15 *him, as though his mercurial nature, his temper, his*
massive dreams and little cruelties, served her only as
sharp reminders of the turbulent longings within him,
longings which she shares but lacks the temperament to
utter and follow to their end.

20 LINDA *(hearing Willy outside the bedroom, calls with*
some trepidation). Willy!
WILLY. It's all right. I came back.

---

  2 **sample case:** Musterkoffer.
  4 **dressed quietly:** unauffällig angezogen.
  7 **the soreness of his palms:** der Schmerz seiner Handflächen.
  8 **word-sigh:** geseufztes Wort; artikulierter Seufzer.
    to escape: hier: entfahren.
 12 **robe:** Bade-, Morgenmantel.
 13 **iron repression:** eiserne Unterdrückung.
    exception to s.th.: Anstoß(nehmen) an etwas.
 15 **mercurial nature:** quecksilbrige, sprunghafte Art.
 17 **longing:** Sehnsucht.
 21 **trepidation:** Besorgtheit.

LINDA. Why? What happened? *(Slight pause.)* Did something happen, Willy?

WILLY. No, nothing happened.

LINDA. You didn't smash the car, did you?

5 WILLY *(with casual irritation)*. I said nothing happened. Didn't you hear me?

LINDA. Don't you feel well?

WILLY. I'm tired to the death. *(The flute has faded away. He sits on the bed beside her, a little numb.)* I couldn't
10 make it. I just couldn't make it, Linda.

LINDA *(very carefully, delicately)*. Where were you all day? You look terrible.

WILLY. I got as far as a little above Yonkers. I stopped for a cup of coffee. Maybe it was the coffee.

15 LINDA. What?

WILLY *(after a pause)*. I suddenly couldn't drive any more. The car kept going off onto the shoulder, y'know?

LINDA *(helpfully)*. Oh. Maybe it was the steering again.
20   I don't think Angelo knows the Studebaker.

WILLY. No, it's me, it's me. Suddenly I realize I'm goin' sixty miles an hour and I don't remember the last five minutes. I'm – I can't seem to – keep my mind to it.

---

4 **to smash:** demolieren, kaputtfahren.
5 **casual:** beiläufig.
8 **to fade away:** allmählich verstummen.
9 **numb:** benommen, starr.
9 f. **I couldn't make it:** Ich hab's nicht geschafft.
11 **delicately** (adv.): hier: feinfühlig, zartfühlend.
13 **Yonkers:** Stadt nördlich von New York.
17 **shoulder:** hier: Bankett, Straßenrand.
19 **steering:** Steuerung.
20 **Studebaker:** amerikanische Automarke.
23 **to keep one's mind to s.th.:** sich auf etwas konzentrieren.

LINDA. Maybe it's your glasses. You never went for your
new glasses.

WILLY. No, I see everything. I came back ten miles an
hour. It took me nearly four hours from Yonkers.

5 LINDA *(resigned)*. Well, you'll just have to take a rest,
Willy, you can't continue this way.

WILLY. I just got back from Florida.

LINDA. But you didn't rest your mind. Your mind is
overactive, and the mind is what counts, dear.

10 WILLY. I'll start out in the morning. Maybe I'll feel
better in the morning. *(She is taking off his shoes.)*
These goddam arch supports are killing me.

LINDA. Take an aspirin. Should I get you an aspirin? It'll
soothe you.

15 WILLY *(with wonder)*. I was driving along, you understand? And I was fine. I was even observing the
scenery. You can imagine, me looking at scenery, on
the road every week of my life. But it's so beautiful
up there, Linda, the trees are so thick, and the sun is
20 warm. I opened the windshield and just let the warm
air bathe over me. And then all of a sudden I'm
goin' off the road! I'm tellin' ya, I absolutely forgot I
was driving. If I'd've gone the other way over the
white line I might've killed somebody. So I went on
25 again – and five minutes later I'm dreamin' again,
and I nearly – *(He presses two fingers against his*

---

12 **goddam** (vulg.): verdammt.
    arch supports: Einlagen zur Unterstützung des Fußristes.
14 **to soothe:** beruhigen.
17 **scenery:** Landschaft.
20 **windshield** (AE): Windschutzscheibe.
21 **all of a sudden:** unerwartet; ganz plötzlich.
22 **ya** (slang): *you.*

eyes.) I have such thoughts, I have such strange thoughts.

LINDA. Willy, dear. Talk to them again. There's no reason why you can't work in New York.

5 WILLY. They don't need me in New York. I'm the New England man. I'm vital in New England.

LINDA. But you're sixty years old. They can't expect you to keep traveling every week.

WILLY. I'll have to send a wire to Portland. I'm supposed
10 to see Brown and Morrison tomorrow morning at ten o'clock to show the line. Goddammit, I could sell them! *(He starts putting on his jacket.)*

LINDA *(taking the jacket from him).* Why don't you go down to the place tomorrow and tell Howard you've
15 simply got to work in New York? You're too accommodating, dear.

WILLY. If old man Wagner was alive I'd a been in charge of New York now! That man was a prince, he was a masterful man. But that boy of his, that Howard, he
20 don't appreciate. When I went north the first time, the Wagner Company didn't know where New England was!

LINDA. Why don't you tell those things to Howard, dear?

25 WILLY *(encouraged).* I will, I definitely will. Is there any cheese?

LINDA. I'll make you a sandwich.

---

11 **line:** hier: Kollektion.
15f. **accommodating:** entgegenkommend.
17 **I'd a been** (coll.): *I would have been.*
17f. **to be in charge of:** verantwortlich sein für.
18 **prince:** hier: nobler Mann.
19 **masterful:** hier: überlegen, souverän.
19f. **he don't:** ungebildet für *he doesn't.*

WILLY. No, go to sleep. I'll take some milk. I'll be up right away. The boys in?

LINDA. They're sleeping. Happy took Biff on a date tonight.

5 WILLY *(interested)*. That so?

LINDA. It was so nice to see them shaving together, one behind the other, in the bathroom. And going out together. You notice? The whole house smells of shaving lotion.

10 WILLY. Figure it out. Work a lifetime to pay off a house. You finally own it, and there's nobody to live in it.

LINDA. Well, dear, life is a casting off. It's always that way.

WILLY. No, no, some people – some people accomplish 15 something. Did Biff say anything after I went this morning?

LINDA. You shouldn't have criticized him, Willy, especially after he just got off the train. You mustn't lose your temper with him.

20 WILLY. When the hell did I lose my temper? I simply asked him if he was making any money. Is that a criticism?

LINDA. But, dear, how could he make any money?

WILLY *(worried and angered)*. There's such an undercur-25 rent in him. He became a moody man. Did he apologize when I left this morning?

---

9 **shaving lotion:** Rasierwasser.
10 **to figure s.th. out:** sich etwas vorstellen, sich eine Vorstellung von etwas machen (AE).
12 **casting off:** hier: Abfallen, Rückgang.
14 f. **to accomplish s.th.:** etwas erreichen (im Leben).
20 **to lose one's temper:** wütend werden; die Geduld verlieren.
24 f. **undercurrent:** hier: unberechenbare (persönliche) Unterströmung.
25 **moody:** launisch.

LINDA. He was crestfallen, Willy. You know how he
admires you. I think if he finds himself, then you'll
both be happier and not fight any more.

WILLY. How can he find himself on a farm? Is that a life?
5   A farmhand? In the beginning, when he was young, I
thought, well, a young man, it's good for him to
tramp around, take a lot of different jobs. But it's
more than ten years now and he has yet to make
thirty-five dollars a week!

10 LINDA. He's finding himself, Willy.

WILLY. Not finding yourself at the age of thirty-four is a
disgrace!

LINDA. Shh!

WILLY. The trouble is he's lazy, goddammit!

15 LINDA. Willy, please!

WILLY. Biff is a lazy bum!

LINDA. They're sleeping. Get something to eat. Go on
down.

WILLY. Why did he come home? I would like to know
20   what brought him home.

LINDA. I don't know. I think he's still lost, Willy. I think
he's very lost.

WILLY. Biff Loman is lost. In the greatest country in the
world a young man with such – personal attractive-
25   ness, gets lost. And such a hard worker. There's one
thing about Biff – he's not lazy.

LINDA. Never.

WILLY *(with pity and resolve)*. I'll see him in the morn-

---

1 **crestfallen:** niedergeschlagen.
5 **farmhand:** Landarbeiter.
7 **to tramp around:** umhervagabundieren.
16 **bum:** Faulpelz, Herumtreiber.
28 **resolve:** Entschlossenheit.

ing; I'll have a nice talk with him. I'll get him a job
selling. He could be big in no time. My God! Remember how they used to follow him around in high
school? When he smiled at one of them their faces lit
up. When he walked down the street . . . *(He loses
himself in reminiscences.)*

LINDA *(trying to bring him out of it)*. Willy, dear, I got
a new kind of American-type cheese today. It's
whipped.

WILLY. Why do you get American when I like Swiss?

LINDA. I just thought you'd like a change –

WILLY. I don't want a change! I want Swiss cheese. Why
am I always being contradicted?

LINDA *(with a covering laugh)*. I thought it would be a
surprise.

WILLY. Why don't you open a window in here, for God's
sake?

LINDA *(with infinite patience)*. They're all open, dear.

WILLY. The way they boxed us in here. Bricks and
windows, windows and bricks.

LINDA. We should've bought the land next door.

WILLY. The street is lined with cars. There's not a breath
of fresh air in the neighborhood. The grass don't
grow any more, you can't raise a carrot in the back
yard. They should've had a law against apartment
houses. Remember those two beautiful elm trees out

---

6 **reminiscence:** Erinnerung.
13 **to contradict:** widersprechen.
14 **covering:** hier: überspielend; ausweichend.
19 **to box s.o. in:** hier: jdn. einmauern, einengen.
22 **breath:** hier: Hauch.
26 **elm tree:** Ulme.

there? When I and Biff hung the swing between
them?

LINDA. Yeah, like being a million miles from the city.

WILLY. They should've arrested the builder for cutting
those down. They massacred the neighborhood.
(Lost.) More and more I think of those days, Linda.
This time of year it was lilac and wisteria. And then
the peonies would come out, and the daffodils. What
fragrance in this room!

LINDA. Well, after all, people had to move somewhere.

WILLY. No, there's more people now.

LINDA. I don't think there's more people. I think –

WILLY. There's more people! That's what's ruining this
country! Population is getting out of control. The
competition is maddening! Smell the stink from that
apartment house! And another one on the other
side . . . How can they whip cheese?
*(On Willy's last line, Biff and Happy raise themselves
up in their beds, listening.)*

LINDA. Go down, try it. And be quiet.

WILLY *(turning to Linda, guiltily)*. You're not worried
about me, are you, sweetheart?

BIFF. What's the matter?

HAPPY. Listen!

---

1 **swing:** Schaukel.
5 **to massacre:** hier: vergewaltigen; zerstören.
7 **lilac:** Flieder.
  wisteria: Glyzine.
8 **peony:** Pfingstrose.
  daffodil: gelbe Narzisse, Osterglocke.
9 **fragrance:** Duft.
15 **to madden:** verrückt, rasend machen.
  stink: Gestank.
21 **guiltily** (adv.): schuldbewußt.

LINDA. You've got too much on the ball to worry about.

WILLY. You're my foundation and my support, Linda.

LINDA. Just try to relax, dear. You make mountains out of molehills.

5 WILLY. I won't fight with him any more. If he wants to go back to Texas, let him go.

LINDA. He'll find his way.

WILLY. Sure. Certain men just don't get started till later in life. Like Thomas Edison, I think. Or B. F. Good-

10 rich. One of them was deaf. *(He starts for the bedroom doorway.)* I'll put my money on Biff.

LINDA. And Willy – if it's warm Sunday we'll drive in the country. And we'll open the windshield, and take lunch.

15 WILLY. No, the windshields don't open on the new cars.

LINDA. But you opened it today.

WILLY. Me? I didn't. *(He stops.)* Now isn't that peculiar! Isn't that a remarkable – *(He breaks off in amazement and fright as the flute is heard distantly.)*

20 LINDA. What, darling?

WILLY. That is the most remarkable thing.

LINDA. What, dear?

WILLY. I was thinking of the Chevvy. *(Slight pause.)*

---

1 **to have s.th. on the ball** (slang; Am. football): eine Menge drauf haben, tüchtig sein.

2 **foundation:** Fundament, Stütze.

3 f. **to make mountains out of molehills:** (fig.) aus einer Mücke einen Elephanten machen (*molehill:* Maulwurfshügel).

9 **Edison:** Thomas Alva E. (1847–1931), berühmter amerikanischer Erfinder.

9 f. **Goodrich:** Benjamin Franklin G. (1841–88), amerikanischer Industrieller.

11 **to put one's money on s.o.:** all sein Geld auf jdn. setzen.

18 **amazement:** Erstaunen.

23 **Chevvy** (coll.): Chevrolet (amerikanische Automarke).

Nineteen twenty-eight . . . when I had that red Chevvy – *(Breaks off.)* That funny? I coulda sworn I was driving that Chevvy today.

LINDA. Well, that's nothing. Something must've reminded you.

WILLY. Remarkable. Ts. Remember those days? The way Biff used to simonize that car? The dealer refused to believe there was eighty thousand miles on it. *(He shakes his head.)* Heh! *(To Linda.)* Close your eyes, I'll be right up. *(He walks out of the bedroom.)*

HAPPY *(to Biff)*. Jesus, maybe he smashed up the car again!

LINDA *(calling after Willy)*. Be careful on the stairs, dear! The cheese is on the middle shelf! *(She turns, goes over to the bed, takes his jacket, and goes out of the bedroom.*

Light has risen on the boys' room. Unseen, Willy is heard talking to himself, "Eighty thousand miles," and a little laugh. Biff gets out of bed, comes downstage a bit, and stands attentively. Biff is two years older than his brother Happy, well built, but in these days bears a worn air and seems less self-assured. He has succeeded less, and his dreams are stronger and less acceptable than Happy's. Happy is tall, powerfully made. Sexuality is like a visible color on him, or a scent that many women have discovered. He, like his brother, is lost, but in a different way, for he has never allowed himself

---

2 **coulda** (slang): *could have.*
7 **to simonize:** polieren (von *Simoniz*, einer Markenpolitur).
22 f. **to bear a worn air:** eine erschöpfte Miene zur Schau tragen.
23 **self-assured:** selbstbewußt; sicher.
26 **scent:** Parfum, Duft.

to turn his face toward defeat and is thus more con-
fused and hard-skinned, although seemingly more
content.)

HAPPY *(getting out of bed)*. He's going to get his license
taken away if he keeps that up. I'm getting nervous
about him, y'know, Biff?

BIFF. His eyes are going.

HAPPY. No, I've driven with him. He sees all right. He
just doesn't keep his mind on it. I drove into the city
with him last week. He stops at a green light and then
it turns red and he goes. *(He laughs.)*

BIFF. Maybe he's color-blind.

HAPPY. Pop? Why he's got the finest eye for color in the
business. You know that.

BIFF *(sitting down on his bed)*. I'm going to sleep.

HAPPY. You're not still sour on Dad, are you, Biff?

BIFF. He's all right, I guess.

WILLY *(underneath them, in the living-room)*. Yes, sir,
eighty thousand miles – eighty-two thousand!

BIFF. You smoking?

HAPPY *(holding out a pack of cigarettes)*. Want one?

BIFF *(taking a cigarette)*. I can never sleep when I smell
it.

WILLY. What a simonizing job, heh!

HAPPY *(with deep sentiment)*. Funny, Biff, y'know? Us
sleeping in here again? The old beds. *(He pats his bed*

---

1 **to turn one's face toward defeat:** der Niederlage ins Gesicht sehen,
  seine Niederlage eingestehen.
2 **hard-skinned:** hartgesotten.
4 **license:** Führerschein.
5 **to keep s.th. up:** etwas so weitermachen.
7 **his eyes are going:** seine Sehkraft läßt stark nach.
13 **pop** (AE): Abk. für *poppa* ›Papa‹.
26 **to pat:** tätscheln.

affectionately.) All the talk that went across those two
beds, huh? Our whole lives.

BIFF. Yeah. Lotta dreams and plans.

HAPPY *(with a deep and masculine laugh).* About five
hundred women would like to know what was said in
this room.

(They share a soft laugh.)

BIFF. Remember that big Betsy something – what the
hell was her name – over on Bushwick Avenue?

HAPPY *(combing his hair).* With the collie dog!

BIFF. That's the one. I got you in there, remember?

HAPPY. Yeah, that was my first time – I think. Boy, there
was a pig! *(They laugh, almost crudely.)* You taught me
everything I know about women. Don't forget that.

BIFF. I bet you forgot how bashful you used to be.
Especially with girls.

HAPPY. Oh, I still am, Biff.

BIFF. Oh, go on.

HAPPY. I just control it, that's all. I think I got less
bashful and you got more so. What happened, Biff?
Where's the old humor, the old confidence? *(He
shakes Biff's knee. Biff gets up and moves restlessly
about the room.)* What's the matter?

BIFF. Why does Dad mock me all the time?

HAPPY. He's not mocking you, he –

BIFF. Everything I say there's a twist of mockery on his
face. I can't get near him.

---

1 **affectionately** (adv.): liebevoll.
3 **lotta** (slang): *a lot of.*
11 **I got you in there:** hier: ich habe dich mit ihr zusammengebracht.
13 **crudely** (adv.): roh, gemein.
15 **bashful:** verschämt; schüchtern.
26 **a twist of mockery:** ein Anflug von Spott.

HAPPY. He just wants you to make good, that's all. I
wanted to talk to you about Dad for a long time, Biff.
Something's – happening to him. He – talks to himself.

5 BIFF. I noticed that this morning. But he always mum-
bled.

HAPPY. But not so noticeable. It got so embarrassing I
sent him to Florida. And you know something? Most
of the time he's talking to you.

10 BIFF. What's he say about me?

HAPPY. I can't make it out.

BIFF. What's he say about me?

HAPPY. I think the fact that you're not settled, that
you're still kind of up in the air . . .

15 BIFF. There's one or two other things depressing him,
Happy.

HAPPY. What do you mean?

BIFF. Never mind. Just don't lay it all to me.

HAPPY. But I think if you just got started – I mean – is
20 there any future for you out there?

BIFF. I tell ya, Hap, I don't know what the future is. I
don't know – what I'm supposed to want.

HAPPY. What do you mean?

BIFF. Well, I spent six or seven years after high school
25 trying to work myself up. Shipping clerk, salesman,
business of one kind or another. And it's a measly
manner of existence. To get on that subway on the
hot mornings in summer. To devote your whole life

5f. **to mumble:** hier: vor sich hin murmeln.
13 **settled:** hier: seßhaft.
18 **don't lay it all to me:** mach mich nicht dafür verantwortlich.
25 **shipping clerk:** Angestellter in der Versandabteilung.
26 **measly:** schäbig, lumpig.

to keeping stock, or making phone calls, or selling or
buying. To suffer fifty weeks of the year for the sake
of a two-week vacation, when all you really desire is
to be outdoors, with your shirt off. And always to
have to get ahead of the next fella. And still – that's
how you build a future.

HAPPY. Well, you really enjoy it on a farm? Are you
content out there?

BIFF *(with rising agitation)*. Hap, I've had twenty or
thirty different kinds of jobs since I left home before
the war, and it always turns out the same. I just
realized it lately. In Nebraska when I herded cattle,
and the Dakotas, and Arizona, and now in Texas.
It's why I came home now, I guess, because I
realized it. This farm I work on, it's spring there
now, see? And they've got about fifteen new colts.
There's nothing more inspiring or – beautiful than
the sight of a mare and a new colt. And it's cool
there now, see? Texas is cool now, and it's spring.
And whenever spring comes to where I am, I suddenly get the feeling, my God, I'm not gettin' anywhere! What the hell am I doing, playing around with
horses, twenty-eight dollars a week! I'm thirty-four
years old, I oughta be makin' my future. That's when
I come running home. And now, I get here, and I
don't know what to do with myself. *(After a pause.)*
I've always made a point of not wasting my life, and

---

1 **to keep stock:** ein Warenlager verwalten.
5 **fella** (slang): *fellow.*
12 **to herd cattle:** Rinder hüten.
16 **colt:** Fohlen.
18 **mare:** Stute.
24 **oughta** (slang): *ought to.*

everytime I come back here I know that all I've done
is to waste my life.

HAPPY. You're a poet, you know that, Biff? You're a –
you're an idealist!

5 BIFF. No, I'm mixed up very bad. Maybe I oughta get
married. Maybe I oughta get stuck into something.
Maybe that's my trouble. I'm like a boy. I'm not
married, I'm not in business, I just – I'm like a boy.
Are you content, Hap? You're a success, aren't you?

10 Are you content?

HAPPY. Hell, no!

BIFF. Why? You're making money, aren't you?

HAPPY *(moving about with energy, expressiveness)*. All I
can do now is wait for the merchandise manager to

15 die. And suppose I get to be merchandise manager?
He's a good friend of mine, and he just built a terrific
estate on Long Island. And he lived there about two
months and sold it, and now he's building another
one. He can't enjoy it once it's finished. And I know

20 that's just what I would do. I don't know what the
hell I'm workin' for. Sometimes I sit in my apartment
– all alone. And I think of the rent I'm paying. And
it's crazy. But then, it's what I always wanted. My
own apartment, a car, and plenty of women. And

25 still, goddammit, I'm lonely.

BIFF *(with enthusiasm)*. Listen, why don't you come out
West with me?

---

5 **mixed up:** durcheinander, verwirrt.
6 **to get stuck into s.th.:** bei einer Sache bleiben.
13 **expressiveness:** Ausdruckskraft.
14 **merchandise manager:** Abteilungsleiter (des An- und Verkaufs).
16 **terrific:** fürchterlich; hier: großartig.
17 **estate:** Landsitz.

HAPPY. You and I, heh?

BIFF. Sure, maybe we could buy a ranch. Raise cattle, use our muscles. Men built like we are should be working out in the open.

5 HAPPY *(avidly)*. The Loman Brothers, heh?

BIFF *(with vast affection)*. Sure, we'd be known all over the counties!

HAPPY *(enthralled)*. That's what I dream about, Biff. Sometimes I want to just rip my clothes off in the

10 middle of the store and outbox that goddam merchandise manager. I mean I can outbox, outrun, and outlift anybody in that store, and I have to take orders from those common, petty sons-of-bitches till I can't stand it any more.

15 BIFF. I'm tellin' you, kid, if you were with me I'd be happy out there.

HAPPY *(enthused)*. See, Biff, everybody around me is so false that I'm constantly lowering my ideals . . .

BIFF. Baby, together we'd stand up for one another,

20 we'd have someone to trust.

HAPPY. If I were around you –

BIFF. Hap, the trouble is we weren't brought up to grub for money. I don't know how to do it.

HAPPY. Neither can I!

---

5 **avidly** (adv.): (be)gierig.
8 **enthralled:** fasziniert; gefesselt.
9 **to rip off:** (vom Leib) reißen.
10 **to outbox s.o.:** jdn. im Boxen schlagen.
13 **petty:** kleinlich.
   sons-of-bitches (vulg.): Hundesöhne, Saukerle.
17 **enthused:** begeistert.
19 **to stand up for:** eintreten für.
22 f. **to grub for s.th.:** nach etwas greifen, grabschen.

BIFF. Then let's go!

HAPPY. The only thing is – what can you make out there?

BIFF. But look at your friend. Builds an estate and then hasn't the peace of mind to live in it.

5 HAPPY. Yeah, but when he walks into the store the waves part in front of him. That's fifty-two thousand dollars a year coming through the revolving door, and I got more in my pinky finger than he's got in his head.

10 BIFF. Yeah, but you just said –

HAPPY. I gotta show some of those pompous, self-important executives over there that Hap Loman can make the grade. I want to walk into the store the way he walks in. Then I'll go with you, Biff.

15 We'll be together yet, I swear. But take those two we had tonight. Now weren't they gorgeous creatures?

BIFF. Yeah, yeah, most gorgeous I've had in years.

HAPPY. I get that any time I want, Biff. Whenever I

20 feel disgusted. The only trouble is, it gets like bowling or something. I just keep knockin' them over and it doesn't mean anything. You still run around a lot?

---

7 **revolving door:** Drehtür.

8 **pinky finger:** kleiner Finger.

11 **gotta** (slang): *got to.*
pompous: hochtrabend, aufgeblasen.

11f. **self-important:** eingebildet.

12 **executive:** leitender Angestellter.

13 **to make the grade:** sich durchsetzen; Erfolg haben; es schaffen.

16 **gorgeous:** prächtig.

20 **disgusted:** angeekelt, angewidert.

21 **I keep knocking them over:** ich lege sie (Mädchen) ständig flach, vernasche sie.

BIFF. Naa. I'd like to find a girl – steady, somebody with
substance.

HAPPY. That's what I long for.

BIFF. Go on! You'd never come home.

5 HAPPY. I would! Somebody with character, with resist-
ance! Like Mom, y'know? You're gonna call me a
bastard when I tell you this. That girl Charlotte I was
with tonight is engaged to be married in five weeks.
(He tries on his new hat.)

10 BIFF. No kiddin'!

HAPPY. Sure, the guy's in line for the vice-presidency of
the store. I don't know what gets into me, maybe I
just have an overdeveloped sense of competition or
something, but I went and ruined her, and further-
15 more I can't get rid of her. And he's the third
executive I've done that to. Isn't that a crummy
characteristic? And to top it all, I go to their wed-
dings! *(Indignantly, but laughing.)* Like I'm not supposed to take bribes. Manufacturers offer me a
20 hundred-dollar bill now and then to throw an order
their way. You know how honest I am, but it's like

---

1 **naa** (slang): *no.*
steady girl: feste Freundin.
6 **gonna** (slang): *going to.*
8 **engaged to be married:** verlobt.
10 **no kiddin'** (coll.): du machst Scherze; du nimmst mich wohl auf die
Schippe.
11 **to be in line for:** Aussicht haben.
16 **crummy** (slang): lausig, dreckig.
17 **to top it all:** allem die Krone aufsetzen.
18 **indignantly** (adv.): entrüstet; unwillig.
19 **bribes:** Bestechungsgelder.
20 f. **to throw an order their way:** ihnen einen Auftrag zukommen
lassen.

this girl, see. I hate myself for it. Because I don't
want the girl, and, still, I take it and – I love it!

BIFF. Let's go to sleep.

HAPPY. I guess we didn't settle anything, heh?

BIFF. I just got one idea that I think I'm going to try.

HAPPY. What's that?

BIFF. Remember Bill Oliver?

HAPPY. Sure, Oliver is very big now. You want to work
for him again?

BIFF. No, but when I quit he said something to me. He
put his arm on my shoulder, and he said, "Biff, if you
ever need anything, come to me."

HAPPY. I remember that. That sounds good.

BIFF. I think I'll go to see him. If I could get ten
thousand or even seven or eight thousand dollars I
could buy a beautiful ranch.

HAPPY. I bet he'd back you. 'Cause he thought highly of
you, Biff. I mean, they all do. You're well liked, Biff.
That's why I say to come back here, and we both have
the apartment. And I'm tellin' you, Biff, any babe
you want . . .

BIFF. No, with a ranch I could do the work I like and still
be something. I just wonder though. I wonder if
Oliver still thinks I stole that carton of basketballs.

HAPPY. Oh, he probably forgot that long ago. It's almost
ten years. You're too sensitive. Anyway, he didn't
really fire you.

BIFF. Well, I think he was going to. I think that's why I
quit. I was never sure whether he knew or not. I

---

10 **to quit:** hier: kündigen; aufhören zu arbeiten.

17 **to back s.o.:** jdn. unterstützen.

20 **babe:** hier: Mädchen.

know he thought the world of me, though. I was the
only one he'd let lock up the place.

WILLY *(below)*. You gonna wash the engine, Biff?

HAPPY. Shh!

5   *(Biff looks at Happy, who is gazing down, listening.
Willy is mumbling in the parlor.)*

HAPPY. You hear that?

(They listen. Willy laughs warmly.)

BIFF *(growing angry)*. Doesn't he know Mom can hear
10   that?

WILLY. Don't get your sweater dirty, Biff!

(A look of pain crosses Biff's face.)

HAPPY. Isn't that terrible? Don't leave again, will you?
You'll find a job here. You gotta stick around. I don't
15   know what to do about him, it's getting embarrassing.

WILLY. What a simonizing job!

BIFF. Mom's hearing that!

WILLY. No kiddin', Biff, you got a date? Wonderful!

HAPPY. Go on to sleep. But talk to him in the morning,
20   will you?

BIFF *(reluctantly getting into bed)*. With her in the house.
Brother!

HAPPY *(getting into bed)*. I wish you'd have a good talk
with him.

25   *(The light on their room begins to fade.)*

BIFF *(to himself in bed)*. That selfish, stupid . . .

HAPPY. Sh . . . Sleep, Biff.

*(Their light is out. Well before they have finished
speaking, Willy's form is dimly seen below in the
30   darkened kitchen. He opens the refrigerator, searches*

---

1 **to think the world of s.o.:** große Stücke auf jdn. halten.
14 **to stick around:** (an einem Ort) bleiben.

*in there, and takes out a bottle of milk. The apartment
houses are fading out, and the entire house and sur-
roundings become covered with leaves. Music insinu-
ates itself as the leaves appear.)*

WILLY. Just wanna be careful with those girls, Biff, that's
all. Don't make any promises. No promises of any
kind. Because a girl, y'know, they always believe
what you tell 'em, and you're very young, Biff, you're
too young to be talking seriously to girls.

*(Light rises on the kitchen. Willy, talking, shuts the
refrigerator door and comes downstage to the kitchen
table. He pours milk into a glass. He is totally
immersed in himself, smiling faintly.)*

WILLY. Too young entirely, Biff. You want to watch your
schooling first. Then when you're all set, there'll be
plenty of girls for a boy like you. *(He smiles broadly at
a kitchen chair.)* That so? The girls pay for you? *(He
laughs.)* Boy, you must really be makin' a hit.

*(Willy is gradually addressing – physically – a point
offstage, speaking through the wall of the kitchen, and
his voice has been rising in volume to that of a normal
conversation.)*

WILLY. I been wondering why you polish the car so
careful. Ha! Don't leave the hubcaps, boys. Get the

---

3 f. **to insinuate o.s.:** hier: leise beginnen, sich bemerkbar machen.
5 **wanna** (slang): *want to.*
13 **to be immersed in o.s.:** in sich selbst versunken sein.
15 **when you're all set:** wenn du fertig bist.
18 **to make a hit:** Erfolg haben.
20 **offstage:** hinter der Bühne.
21 **volume:** Lautstärke.
24 **hubcap:** Radkappe.

chamois to the hubcaps. Happy, use newspaper on
the windows, it's the easiest thing. Show him how to
do it, Biff! You see, Happy? Pad it up, use it like a
pad. That's it, that's it, good work. You're doin' all
5   right, Hap. *(He pauses, then nods in approbation for
a few seconds, then looks upward.)* Biff, first thing
we gotta do when we get time is clip that big branch
over the house. Afraid it's gonna fall in a storm and
hit the roof. Tell you what. We get a rope and sling
10   her around, and then we climb up there with a
couple of saws and take her down. Soon as you finish
the car, boys, I wanna see ya. I got a surprise for you,
boys.

BIFF *(offstage)*. Whatta ya got, Dad?

15   WILLY. No, you finish first. Never leave a job till you're
finished – remember that. *(Looking toward the "big
trees".)* Biff, up in Albany I saw a beautiful hammock. I think I'll buy it next trip, and we'll hang it
right between those two elms. Wouldn't that be
20   something? Just swingin' there under those branches.
Boy, that would be . . .

*(Young Biff and Young Happy appear from the direc-
tion Willy was addressing. Happy carries rags and a
pail of water. Biff, wearing a sweater with a block "S,"*
25   *carries a football.)*

---

1 **chamois:** Lederlappen.
3 **to pad:** zusammenknüllen.
4 **pad:** Polierkissen; dicker Lappen.
5 **to nod in approbation:** zustimmend nicken.
7 **to clip:** abschneiden; stutzen.
14 **whatta ya got** (*slang*): *what have you got*.
17 f. **hammock:** Hängematte.
24 **block** (*letter*): Großbuchstabe.

BIFF *(pointing in the direction of the car offstage)*. How's that, Pop, professional?

WILLY. Terrific. Terrific job, boys. Good work, Biff.

HAPPY. Where's the surprise, Pop?

5 WILLY. In the back seat of the car.

HAPPY. Boy! *(He runs off.)*

BIFF. What is it, Dad? Tell me, what'd you buy?

WILLY *(laughing, cuffs him)*. Never mind, something I want you to have.

10 BIFF *(turns and starts off)*. What is it, Hap?

HAPPY *(offstage)*. It's a punching bag!

BIFF. Oh, Pop!

WILLY. It's got Gene Tunney's signature on it!

(Happy runs onstage with a punching bag.)

15 BIFF. Gee, how'd you know we wanted a punching bag?

WILLY. Well, it's the finest thing for the timing.

HAPPY *(lies down on his back and pedals with his feet)*. I'm losing weight, you notice, Pop?

WILLY *(to Happy)*. Jumping rope is good too.

20 BIFF. Did you see the new football I got?

WILLY *(examining the ball)*. Where'd you get a new ball?

BIFF. The coach told me to practice my passing.

WILLY. That so? And he gave you the ball, heh?

---

8 **to cuff:** knuffen.

11 **punching bag:** Sandsack (Übungsgerät für Boxer).

13 **Gene Tunney:** James Joseph T. (berühmter Boxer, Schwergewichtsweltmeister 1926–28).

15 **gee:** Ausruf des Erstaunens, Entzückens.

16 **timing:** zeitliche Abstimmung; Bewegungskoordination.

17 **to pedal:** hier: in der Luft radfahren.

23 **coach:** Trainer.

   to pass (Am. football): den Ball zu einem Mitspieler werfen.

BIFF. Well, I borrowed it from the locker room. *(He laughs confidentially.)*

WILLY *(laughing with him at the theft)*. I want you to return that.

5 HAPPY. I told you he wouldn't like it!

BIFF *(angrily)*. Well, I'm bringing it back!

WILLY *(stopping the incipient argument, to Happy)*. Sure, he's gotta practice with a regulation ball, doesn't he? *(To Biff.)* Coach'll probably congratulate
10 you on your initiative!

BIFF. Oh, he keeps congratulating my initiative all the time, Pop.

WILLY. That's because he likes you. If somebody else took that ball there'd be an uproar. So what's the
15 report, boys, what's the report?

BIFF. Where'd you go this time, Dad? Gee we were lonesome for you.

WILLY *(pleased, puts an arm around each boy and they come down to the apron)*. Lonesome, heh?

20 BIFF. Missed you every minute.

WILLY. Don't say? Tell you a secret, boys. Don't breathe it to a soul. Someday I'll have my own business, and I'll never have to leave home any more.

HAPPY. Like Uncle Charley, heh?

25 WILLY. Bigger than Uncle Charley! Because Charley is not – liked. He's liked, but he's not – well liked.

---

1 **locker room:** Umkleideraum (mit Schließfächern).
3 **theft:** Diebstahl.
7 **incipient argument:** hier: beginnender Streit.
8 **regulation ball:** Ball, der den Vorschriften entspricht.
10 **initiative:** Initiative; Eifer.
14 **uproar:** Krach; Aufruhr.
16 f. **to be lonesome for s.o.:** jdn. vermissen.
21 f. **don't breathe it to a soul:** verrate(t) es niemandem.

BIFF. Where'd you go this time, Dad?

WILLY. Well, I got on the road, and I went north to Providence. Met the Mayor.

BIFF. The Mayor of Providence!

5 WILLY. He was sitting in the hotel lobby.

BIFF. What'd he say?

WILLY. He said, "Morning!" And I said, "You got a fine city here, Mayor." And then he had coffee with me. And then I went to Waterbury. Waterbury is a fine
10 city. Big clock city, the famous Waterbury clock. Sold a nice bill there. And then Boston – Boston is the cradle of the Revolution. A fine city. And a couple of other towns in Mass., and on to Portland and Bangor and straight home!

15 BIFF. Gee, I'd love to go with you sometime, Dad.

WILLY. Soon as summer comes.

HAPPY. Promise?

WILLY. You and Hap and I, and I'll show you all the towns. America is full of beautiful towns and fine,
20 upstanding people. And they know me, boys, they know me up and down New England. The finest people. And when I bring you fellas up, there'll be open sesame for all of us, 'cause one thing, boys: I have friends. I can park my car in any street in New
25 England, and the cops protect it like their own. This summer, heh?

BIFF and HAPPY *(together)*. Yeah! You bet!

---

5 **hotel lobby:** Hotelhalle; Foyer.
10f. **to sell a nice bill:** eine hübsche Summe umsetzen.
12 **cradle:** Wiege.
20 **upstanding people:** aufrechte Leute.
23 **open sesame:** Sesam-öffne-dich; offene Türen.
25 **cop** (slang): Polizist.
27 **you bet!:** hier: au ja!

WILLY. We'll take our bathing suits.

HAPPY. We'll carry your bags, Pop!

WILLY. Oh, won't that be something! Me comin' into the
Boston stores with you boys carryin' my bags. What a
5   sensation!

(Biff is prancing around, practicing passing the ball.)

WILLY. You nervous, Biff, about the game?

BIFF. Not if you're gonna be there.

WILLY. What do they say about you in school, now that
10   they made you captain?

HAPPY. There's a crowd of girls behind him everytime
the classes change.

BIFF *(taking Willy's hand)*. This Saturday, Pop, this
Saturday – just for you, I'm going to break through
15   for a touchdown.

HAPPY. You're supposed to pass.

BIFF. I'm takin' one play for Pop. You watch me, Pop,
and when I take off my helmet, that means I'm
breakin' out. Then you watch me crash through that
20   line!

WILLY *(kisses Biff)*. Oh, wait'll I tell this in Boston!

*(Bernard enters in knickers. He is younger than Biff,
earnest and loyal, a worried boy.)*

BERNARD. Biff, where are you? You're supposed to
25   study with me today.

WILLY. Hey, looka Bernard. What're you lookin' so
anemic about, Bernard?

---

6 **to prance:** umhertänzeln.

14f. **to break through for a touchdown** (Am. football): die Abwehr
durchbrechen, um den Ball hinter die gegnerische Torlinie zu
bringen.

20 **line** (Am. football): Verteidigungslinie, Abwehrreihe.

22 **knickers** (pl.): Abk. für *knickerbockers* ›Kniebundhose‹.

27 **anemic:** blutarm; schlapp.

BERNARD. He's gotta study, Uncle Willy. He's got Regents next week.

HAPPY *(tauntingly, spinning Bernard around)*. Let's box, Bernard!

5 BERNARD. Biff! *(He gets away from Happy.)* Listen, Biff, I heard Mr. Birnbaum say that if you don't start studyin' math he's gonna flunk you, and you won't graduate. I heard him!

WILLY. You better study with him, Biff. Go ahead now.

10 BERNARD. I heard him!

BIFF. Oh, Pop, you didn't see my sneakers! *(He holds up a foot for Willy to look at.)*

WILLY. Hey, that's a beautiful job of printing!

BERNARD *(wiping his glasses)*. Just because he printed
15 University of Virginia on his sneakers doesn't mean they've got to graduate him, Uncle Willy!

WILLY *(angrily)*. What're you talking about? With scholarships to three universities they're gonna flunk him?

BERNARD. But I heard Mr. Birnbaum say –

20 WILLY. Don't be a pest, Bernard! *(To his boys.)* What an anemic!

BERNARD. Okay, I'm waiting for you in my house, Biff. *(Bernard goes off. The Lomans laugh.)*

WILLY. Bernard is not well liked, is he?

25 BIFF. He's liked, but he's not well liked.

---

2 **Regents:** spezielle Form des Examens *(regent:* Mitglied des Aufsichtskomitees einer Schule oder Universität).

3 **taunting:** spöttisch.
  to spin around: herumwirbeln.

7 **to flunk s.o.:** jdn. durchfallen lassen.

8 **to graduate:** das Abschlußexamen machen.

11 **sneakers** (AE, coll.): Turnschuhe.

17 f. **scholarship:** Stipendium.

20 **don't be a pest:** geh mir nicht auf die Nerven.

HAPPY. That's right, Pop.

WILLY. That's just what I mean. Bernard can get the best
marks in school, y'understand, but when he gets out
in the business world, y'understand, you are going to
5 be five times ahead of him. That's why I thank
Almighty God you're both built like Adonises.
Because the man who makes an appearance in the
business world, the man who creates personal interest, is the man who gets ahead. Be liked and you will
10 never want. You take me, for instance. I never have
to wait in line to see a buyer. "Willy Loman is here!"
That's all they have to know, and I go right through.

BIFF. Did you knock them dead, Pop?

WILLY. Knocked 'em cold in Providence, slaughtered
15 'em in Boston.

HAPPY *(on his back, pedaling again)*. I'm losing weight,
you notice, Pop?
*(Linda enters, as of old, a ribbon in her hair, carrying
a basket of washing.)*
20 LINDA *(with youthful energy)*. Hello, dear!

WILLY. Sweetheart!

LINDA. How'd the Chevvy run?

WILLY. Chevrolet, Linda, is the greatest car ever built.
(To the boys.) Since when do you let your mother
25 carry wash up the stairs?

---

6 **Adonis:** in der griechischen Sage Geliebter der Aphrodite; danach:
schöner Jüngling.
9 **to get ahead:** hier: vorankommen; es zu etwas bringen.
9 f. **you will never want:** dir wird's an nichts fehlen.
13/14 **to knock s.o. dead/cold:** jdn. auspunkten; hier: im Geschäftsleben
übertrumpfen.
14 **to slaughter:** schlachten; hier: Steigerung zu *to knock s.o. dead/cold.*
18 **as of old:** wie ehemals.

BIFF. Grab hold there, boy!

HAPPY. Where to, Mom?

LINDA. Hang them up on the line. And you better go
down to your friends, Biff. The cellar is full of boys.
5 They don't know what to do with themselves.

BIFF. Ah, when Pop comes home they can wait!

WILLY *(laughs appreciatively)*. You better go down and
tell them what to do, Biff.

BIFF. I think I'll have them sweep out the furnace room.

10 WILLY. Good work, Biff.

BIFF *(goes through wall-line of kitchen to doorway at
back and calls down)*. Fellas! Everybody sweep out
the furnace room! I'll be right down!

VOICES. All right! Okay, Biff.

15 BIFF. George and Sam and Frank, come out back! We're
hangin' up the wash! Come on, Hap, on the double!
(He and Happy carry out the basket.)

LINDA. The way they obey him!

WILLY. Well, that's training, the training. I'm tellin' you,
20 I was sellin' thousands and thousands, but I had to
come home.

LINDA. Oh, the whole block'll be at that game. Did you
sell anything?

WILLY. I did five hundred gross in Providence and seven
25 hundred gross in Boston.

LINDA. No! Wait a minute, I've got a pencil. *(She pulls
pencil and paper out of her apron pocket.)* That

---

1 **grab hold:** pack an!
7 **appreciatively** (adv.): verständnisvoll; anerkennend.
9 **furnace room:** Heizungskeller, Heizraum.
16 **on the double** (milit.): schneller; mit größerem Tempo.
24 **gross:** Brutto, Gesamtumsatz.

makes your commission . . . Two hundred – my God!
Two hundred and twelve dollars!

WILLY. Well, I didn't figure it yet, but . . .

LINDA. How much did you do?

5 WILLY. Well, I – I did – about a hundred and eighty gross
in Providence. Well, no – it came to – roughly two
hundred gross on the whole trip.

LINDA *(without hesitation)*. Two hundred gross. That's
. . . *(She figures.)*

10 WILLY. The trouble was that three of the stores were half
closed for inventory in Boston. Otherwise I woulda
broke records.

LINDA. Well, it makes seventy dollars and some pennies.
That's very good.

15 WILLY. What do we owe?

LINDA. Well, on the first there's sixteen dollars on the
refrigerator –

WILLY. Why sixteen?

LINDA. Well, the fan belt broke, so it was a dollar eighty.

20 WILLY. But it's brand new.

LINDA. Well, the man said that's the way it is. Till they
work themselves in, y'know.

(They move through the wall-line into the kitchen.)

WILLY. I hope we didn't get stuck on that machine.

25 LINDA. They got the biggest ads of any of them!

---

1 **commission:** Provision.
11 **inventory:** Inventur.
12 **broke** (arch.): *broken.*
19 **fan belt:** Ventilatorriemen.
20 **brand new:** nagelneu.
24 **to get stuck on s.th.:** auf etwas sitzenbleiben; mit etwas reingelegt
werden.
25 **ad:** Abk. für *advertisement* ›Reklame‹.

WILLY. I know, it's a fine machine. What else?

LINDA. Well, there's nine-sixty for the washing machine.
And for the vacuum cleaner there's three and a half
due on the fifteenth. Then the roof, you got twenty-
one dollars remaining.

WILLY. It don't leak, does it?

LINDA. No, they did a wonderful job. Then you owe
Frank for the carburetor.

WILLY. I'm not going to pay that man! That goddam
Chevrolet, they ought to prohibit the manufacture of
that car!

LINDA. Well, you owe him three and a half. And odds
and ends, comes to around a hundred and twenty
dollars by the fifteenth.

WILLY. A hundred and twenty dollars! My God, if
business don't pick up I don't know what I'm gonna
do!

LINDA. Well, next week you'll do better.

WILLY. Oh, I'll knock 'em dead next week. I'll go to
Hartford. I'm very well liked in Hartford. You know,
the trouble is, Linda, people don't seem to take to
me.
(They move onto the forestage.)

LINDA. Oh, don't be foolish.

WILLY. I know it when I walk in. They seem to laugh at
me.

---

3 **vacuum cleaner:** Staubsauger.

6 **to leak:** lecken, ein Loch haben.

8 **carburetor:** Vergaser.

12 f. **odds and ends:** allerlei Kleinigkeiten; Krimskrams.

15 f. **if business don't pick up:** wenn das Geschäft nicht besser geht.

21 f. **to take to s.o.:** jdn. sympathisch finden.

LINDA. Why? Why would they laugh at you? Don't talk
that way, Willy.

*(Willy moves to the edge of the stage. Linda goes into
the kitchen and starts to darn stockings.)*

5 WILLY. I don't know the reason for it, but they just pass
me by. I'm not noticed.

LINDA. But you're doing wonderful, dear. You're making seventy to a hundred dollars a week.

WILLY. But I gotta be at it ten, twelve hours a day. Other
10 men – I don't know – they do it easier. I don't know
why – I can't stop myself – I talk too much. A man
oughta come in with a few words. One thing about
Charley. He's a man of few words, and they respect
him.

15 LINDA. You don't talk too much, you're just lively.

WILLY *(smiling)*. Well, I figure, what the hell, life is
short, a couple of jokes. *(To himself.)* I joke too
much! *(The smile goes.)*

LINDA. Why? You're –

20 WILLY. I'm fat. I'm very – foolish to look at, Linda. I
didn't tell you, but Christmas time I happened to
be calling on F. H. Stewarts, and a salesman I know,
as I was going in to see the buyer I heard him say
something about – walrus. And I – I cracked him
25 right across the face. I won't take that. I simply
will not take that. But they do laugh at me. I know
that.

LINDA. Darling . . .

---

4 **to darn:** stopfen.

5f. **to pass s.o. by:** jdn. übergehen, übersehen.

24 **walrus:** Walroß.

24f. **to crack s.o. across the face:** jdm. eine langen, einen Schlag ins
Gesicht geben.

WILLY. I gotta overcome it. I know I gotta overcome it.
I'm not dressing to advantage, maybe.

LINDA. Willy, darling, you're the handsomest man in the
world –

5 WILLY. Oh, no, Linda.

LINDA. To me you are. *(Slight pause.)* The handsomest.
*(From the darkness is heard the laughter of a woman.
Willy doesn't turn to it, but it continues through Lin-
da's lines.)*

10 LINDA. And the boys, Willy. Few men are idolized by
their children the way you are.
*(Music is heard as behind a scrim, to the left of the
house, The Woman, dimly seen, is dressing.)*

WILLY *(with great feeling).* You're the best there is,

15 Linda, you're a pal, you know that? On the road – on
the road I want to grab you sometimes and just kiss
the life outa you.
*(The laughter is loud now, and he moves into a
brightening area at the left, where The Woman has*

20 *come from behind the scrim and is standing, putting
on her hat, looking into a "mirror" and laughing.)*

WILLY. 'Cause I get so lonely – especially when business
is bad and there's nobody to talk to. I get the feeling
that I'll never sell anything again, that I won't make a

25 living for you, or a business, a business for the boys.
*(He talks through The Woman's subsiding laughter!
The Woman primps at the "mirror.")* There's so much
I want to make for –

---

2 **to dress to advantage:** sich vorteilhaft kleiden.
10 **to idolize:** abgöttisch verehren.
12 **scrim:** Baumwollstoff; hier: Vorhang, Paravent.
15 **pal** (coll.): guter Kamerad, Kumpel.
26 **to subside:** nachlassen.
27 **to primp:** sich geziert betrachten.

THE WOMAN. Me? You didn't make me, Willy. I picked you.

WILLY *(pleased).* You picked me?

THE WOMAN *(who is quite proper-looking, Willy's age).* I did. I've been sitting at that desk watching all the salesmen go by, day in, day out. But you've got such a sense of humor, and we do have such a good time together, don't we?

WILLY. Sure, sure. *(He takes her in his arms.)* Why do you have to go now?

THE WOMAN. It's two o'clock ...

WILLY. No, come on in! *(He pulls her.)*

THE WOMAN. ... my sisters'll be scandalized. When'll you be back?

WILLY. Oh, two weeks about. Will you come up again?

THE WOMAN. Sure thing. You do make me laugh. It's good for me. *(She squeezes his arm, kisses him.)* And I think you're a wonderful man.

WILLY. You picked me, heh?

THE WOMAN. Sure. Because you're so sweet. And such a kidder.

WILLY. Well, I'll see you next time I'm in Boston.

THE WOMAN. I'll put you right through to the buyers.

WILLY *(slapping her bottom).* Right. Well, bottoms up!

THE WOMAN *(slaps him gently and laughs).* You just kill me, Willy. *(He suddenly grabs her and kisses her*

1f. **to pick s.o.:** jdn. aussuchen.
13 **scandalized:** empört, entrüstet.
21 **kidder** (coll.): Spaßvogel.
24 **to slap:** einen Klaps geben.
   bottoms up: Prost, hoch die Tassen; hier: Anspielung auf *bottom* ›Hinterteil‹.
25f. **you just kill me:** hier: du bist so komisch.

roughly.) You kill me. And thanks for the stockings.
I love a lot of stockings. Well, good night.

WILLY. Good night. And keep your pores open!

THE WOMAN. Oh, Willy!

5 *(The Woman bursts out laughing, and Linda's laughter blends in. The Woman disappears into the dark.
Now the area at the kitchen table brightens. Linda is
sitting where she was at the kitchen table, but now is
mending a pair of her silk stockings.)*

10 LINDA. You are, Willy. The handsomest man. You've
got no reason to feel that –

WILLY *(coming out of The Woman's dimming area and
going over to Linda)*. I'll make it all up to you, Linda,
I'll –

15 LINDA. There's nothing to make up, dear. You're doing
fine, better than –

WILLY *(noticing her mending)*. What's that?

LINDA. Just mending my stockings. They're so expen-
sive –

20 WILLY *(angrily, taking them from her)*. I won't have you
mending stockings in this house! Now throw them
out!

(Linda puts the stockings in her pocket.)

BERNARD *(entering on the run)*. Where is he? If he

25 doesn't study!

WILLY *(moving to the forestage, with great agitation)*.
You'll give him the answers!

BERNARD. I do, but I can't on a Regents! That's a state
exam! They're liable to arrest me!

30 WILLY.Where is he? I'll whip him, I'll whip him!

3 **keep your pores open:** (fig.) bleib wachsam.

LINDA. And he'd better give back that football, Willy,
it's not nice.

WILLY. Biff! Where is he? Why is he taking everything?

LINDA. He's too rough with the girls, Willy. All the
5   mothers are afraid of him!

WILLY. I'll whip him!

BERNARD. He's driving the car without a license!

(The Woman's laugh is heard.)

WILLY. Shut up!

10   LINDA. All the mothers –

WILLY. Shut up!

BERNARD *(backing quietly away and out)*. Mr. Birnbaum
says he's stuck up.

WILLY. Get outa here!

15   BERNARD. If he doesn't buckle down he'll flunk math!

(He goes off.)

LINDA. He's right, Willy, you've gotta –

WILLY *(exploding at her)*. There's nothing the matter
with him! You want him to be a worm like Bernard?

20   He's got spirit, personality . . .

*(As he speaks, Linda, almost in tears, exits into the
living-room. Willy is alone in the kitchen, wilting and
staring. The leaves are gone. It is night again, and the
apartment houses look down from behind.)*

25   WILLY. Loaded with it. Loaded! What is he stealing?
He's giving it back, isn't he? Why is he stealing?
What did I tell him? I never in my life told him
anything but decent things.

---

13 **to be stuck up:** eingebildet, überheblich sein.
15 **to buckle down:** sich ernstlich an die Arbeit machen.
21 **to exit:** abgehen (von der Bühne).
22 **to wilt:** hier: den Kopf hängen lassen; in sich zusammensinken.

(Happy in pajamas has come down the stairs; Willy suddenly becomes aware of Happy's presence.)

HAPPY. Let's go now, come on.

WILLY *(sitting down at the kitchen table)*. Huh! Why did she have to wax the floors herself? Everytime she waxes the floors she keels over. She knows that!

HAPPY. Shh! Take it easy. What brought you back tonight?

WILLY. I got an awful scare. Nearly hit a kid in Yonkers. God! Why didn't I go to Alaska with my brother Ben that time! Ben! That man was a genius, that man was success incarnate! What a mistake! He begged me to go.

HAPPY. Well, there's no use in –

WILLY. You guys! There was a man started with the clothes on his back and ended up with diamond mines!

HAPPY. Boy, someday I'd like to know how he did it.

WILLY. What's the mystery? The man knew what he wanted and went out and got it! Walked into a jungle, and comes out, the age of twenty-one, and he's rich! The world is an oyster, but you don't crack it open on a mattress!

HAPPY. Pop, I told you I'm gonna retire you for life.

---

5 **to wax:** bohnern.
6 **to keel over:** umkippen.
9 **scare:** Schrecken.
12 **success incarnate:** Erfolg in Menschengestalt.
15 **guy** (slang): Bursche, Kerl.
20 **jungle:** Dschungel.
22 **oyster:** Auster.
23 **mattress:** Matratze.
24 **to retire s.o.:** hier: jdm. den Ruhestand ermöglichen.

WILLY. You'll retire me for life on seventy goddam
dollars a week? And your women and your car and
your apartment, and you'll retire me for life! Christ's
sake, I couldn't get past Yonkers today! Where are
you guys, where are you? The woods are burning! I
can't drive a car!

*(Charley has appeared in the doorway. He is a large
man, slow of speech, laconic, immovable. In all he
says, despite what he says, there is pity, and, now,
trepidation. He has a robe over pajamas, slippers on
his feet. He enters the kitchen.)*

CHARLEY. Everything all right?

HAPPY. Yeah, Charley, everything's . . .

WILLY. What's the matter?

CHARLEY. I heard some noise. I thought something
happened. Can't we do something about the walls?
You sneeze in here, and in my house hats blow off.

HAPPY. Let's go to bed, Dad. Come on.

(Charley signals to Happy to go.)

WILLY. You go ahead, I'm not tired at the moment.

HAPPY *(to Willy)*. Take it easy, huh? *(He exits.)*

WILLY. What're you doin' up?

CHARLEY *(sitting down at the kitchen table opposite
Willy)*. Couldn't sleep good. I had a heartburn.

WILLY. Well, you don't know how to eat.

CHARLEY. I eat with my mouth.

WILLY. No, you're ignorant. You gotta know about
vitamins and things like that.

---

8 **laconic:** einsilbig.
  immovable: unbeweglich.
17 **to sneeze:** niesen.
24 **heartburn:** Sodbrennen.

CHARLEY. Come on, let's shoot. Tire you out a little.

WILLY *(hesitantly)*. All right. You got cards?

CHARLEY *(taking a deck from his pocket)*. Yeah, I got them. Someplace. What is it with those vitamins?

5 WILLY *(dealing)*. They build up your bones. Chemistry.

CHARLEY. Yeah, but there's no bones in a heartburn.

WILLY. What are you talkin' about? Do you know the first thing about it?

10 CHARLEY. Don't get insulted.

WILLY. Don't talk about something you don't know anything about.

(They are playing. Pause.)

CHARLEY. What're you doin' home?

15 WILLY. A little trouble with the car.

CHARLEY. Oh. *(Pause.)* I'd like to take a trip to California.

WILLY. Don't say.

CHARLEY. You want a job?

20 WILLY. I got a job, I told you that. *(After a slight pause.)* What the hell are you offering me a job for?

CHARLEY. Don't get insulted.

WILLY. Don't insult me.

CHARLEY. I don't see no sense in it. You don't have to go
25 on this way.

WILLY. I got a good job. *(Slight pause.)* What do you keep comin' in here for?

CHARLEY. You want me to go?

---

1 **let's shoot:** laß uns ein Spielchen machen.

3 **deck:** Kartenspiel.

5 **to deal:** hier: (Karten) austeilen.

18 **don't say** (coll.): was du nicht sagst.

WILLY *(after a pause, withering)*. I can't understand it.
He's going back to Texas again. What the hell is that?

CHARLEY. Let him go.

WILLY. I got nothin' to give him, Charley, I'm clean, I'm
clean.

CHARLEY. He won't starve. None a them starve. Forget
about him.

WILLY. Then what have I got to remember?

CHARLEY. You take it too hard. To hell with it. When a
deposit bottle is broken you don't get your nickel
back.

WILLY. That's easy enough for you to say.

CHARLEY. That ain't easy for me to say.

WILLY. Did you see the ceiling I put up in the living-
room?

CHARLEY. Yeah, that's a piece of work. To put up a
ceiling is a mystery to me. How do you do it?

WILLY. What's the difference?

CHARLEY. Well, talk about it.

WILLY. You gonna put up a ceiling?

CHARLEY. How could I put up a ceiling?

WILLY. Then what the hell are you bothering me for?

CHARLEY. You're insulted again.

WILLY. A man who can't handle tools is not a man.
You're disgusting.

CHARLEY. Don't call me disgusting, Willy.

---

1 **withering:** hier: niedergeschlagen; mutlos.
4f. **clean** (coll.): blank; pleite.
6 **a them** (slang): *of them*.
10 **deposit bottle:** Pfandflasche.
  nickel (coll.): Münze (5 *cents*).
13 **ain't** (slang): *isn't*.
26 **disgusting:** ekelhaft, widerwärtig.

(Uncle Ben, carrying a valise and an umbrella, enters the forestage from around the right corner of the house. He is a stolid man, in his sixties, with a mustache and an authoritative air. He is utterly certain of his destiny, and there is an aura of far places about him. He enters exactly as Willy speaks.)

WILLY. I'm getting awfully tired, Ben.

(Ben's music is heard. Ben looks around at everything.)

CHARLEY. Good, keep playing; you'll sleep better. Did you call me Ben?

(Ben looks at his watch.)

WILLY. That's funny. For a second there you reminded me of my brother Ben.

BEN. I only have a few minutes. *(He strolls, inspecting the place. Willy and Charley continue playing.)*

CHARLEY. You never heard from him again, heh? Since that time?

WILLY. Didn't Linda tell you? Couple of weeks ago we got a letter from his wife in Africa. He died.

CHARLEY. That so.

BEN *(chuckling)*. So this is Brooklyn, eh?

CHARLEY. Maybe you're in for some of his money.

WILLY. Naa, he had seven sons. There's just one opportunity I had with that man . . .

BEN. I must make a train, William. There are several properties I'm looking at in Alaska.

---

1 **valise:** Handkoffer, Reisetasche.
3 **stolid:** unempfindlich; gleichmütig.
4 **authoritative air:** gebieterische Miene.
5 **aura:** Aura; Atmosphäre.
22 **to chuckle:** kichern.
23 **to be in for s.th.:** auf etwas Aussicht haben.

WILLY. Sure, sure! If I'd gone with him to Alaska that time, everything would've been totally different.

CHARLEY. Go on, you'd froze to death up there.

WILLY. What're you talking about?

5 BEN. Opportunity is tremendous in Alaska, William. Surprised you're not up there.

WILLY. Sure, tremendous.

CHARLEY. Heh?

WILLY. There was the only man I ever met who knew the
10 answers.

CHARLEY. Who?

BEN. How are you all?

WILLY *(taking a pot, smiling)*. Fine, fine.

CHARLEY. Pretty sharp tonight.

15 BEN. Is Mother living with you?

WILLY. No, she died a long time ago.

CHARLEY. Who?

BEN. That's too bad. Fine specimen of a lady, Mother.

WILLY *(to Charley)*. Heh?

20 BEN. I'd hoped to see the old girl.

CHARLEY. Who died?

BEN. Heard anything from Father, have you?

WILLY *(unnerved)*. What do you mean, who died?

CHARLEY *(taking a pot)*. What're you talkin' about?

25 BEN *(looking at his watch)*. William, it's half-past eight!

WILLY *(as though to dispel his confusion he angrily stops Charley's hand)*. That's my build!

---

3 **froze:** Part. Perf. von *to freeze*.
13 **pot:** Gewinn beim Spiel; Einsatz.
18 **specimen:** Muster, Exemplar.
23 **to unnerve:** entnerven; zermürben.
26 **to dispel:** zerstreuen, vertreiben.
27 **that's my build:** das ist meine Serie, mein Stich (und daher: mein Topf).

CHARLEY. I put the ace –

WILLY. If you don't know how to play the game I'm not gonna throw my money away on you!

CHARLEY *(rising)*. It was my ace, for God's sake!

5 WILLY. I'm through, I'm through!

BEN. When did Mother die?

WILLY. Long ago. Since the beginning you never knew how to play cards.

CHARLEY *(picks up the cards and goes to the door)*. All

10 right! Next time I'll bring a deck with five aces.

WILLY. I don't play that kind of game!

CHARLEY *(turning to him)*. You ought to be ashamed of yourself!

WILLY. Yeah?

15 CHARLEY. Yeah! *(He goes out.)*

WILLY *(slamming the door after him)*. Ignoramus!

BEN *(as Willy comes toward him through the wall-line of the kitchen)*. So you're William.

WILLY *(shaking Ben's hand)*. Ben! I've been waiting for

20 you so long! What's the answer? How did you do it?

BEN. Oh, there's a story in that.

(Linda enters the forestage, as of old, carrying the wash basket.)

LINDA. Is this Ben?

25 BEN *(gallantly)*. How do you do, my dear.

LINDA. Where've you been all these years? Willy's always wondered why you –

WILLY *(pulling Ben away from her impatiently)*. Where

---

1 **ace:** As (Kartenspiel).

5 **I'm through:** Schluß jetzt; ich hab genug.

16 **to slam:** (zu)knallen.

   ignoramus: Ignorant; Dummkopf.

25 **gallantly** *(adv.)*: galant.

is Dad? Didn't you follow him? How did you get
started?

BEN. Well, I don't know how much you remember.

WILLY. Well, I was just a baby, of course, only three or
5   four years old –

BEN. Three years and eleven months.

WILLY. What a memory, Ben!

BEN. I have many enterprises, William, and I have never
kept books.

10   WILLY. I remember I was sitting under the wagon in –
was it Nebraska?

BEN. It was South Dakota, and I gave you a bunch of
wild flowers.

WILLY. I remember you walking away down some open
15   road.

BEN *(laughing).* I was going to find Father in Alaska.

WILLY. Where is he?

BEN. At that age I had a very faulty view of geography,
William. I discovered after a few days that I was
20   heading due south, so instead of Alaska, I ended up
in Africa.

LINDA. Africa!

WILLY. The Gold Coast!

BEN. Principally diamond mines.

25   LINDA. Diamond mines!

BEN. Yes, my dear. But I've only a few minutes –

WILLY. No! Boys! Boys! *(Young Biff and Happy
appear.)* Listen to this. This is your Uncle Ben, a
great man! Tell my boys, Ben!

---

9 **to keep books:** Buch führen.
18 **faulty:** fehlerhaft; unzulänglich.
20 **to head due south:** genau nach Süden gehen.

BEN. Why, boys, when I was seventeen I walked into the
jungle, and when I was twenty-one I walked out. *(He
laughs.)* And by God I was rich.

WILLY *(to the boys).* You see what I been talking about?
The greatest things can happen!

BEN *(glancing at his watch).* I have an appointment in
Ketchikan Tuesday week.

WILLY. No, Ben! Please tell about Dad. I want my boys
to hear. I want them to know the kind of stock they
spring from. All I remember is a man with a big
beard, and I was in Mamma's lap, sitting around a
fire, and some kind of high music.

BEN. His flute. He played the flute.

WILLY. Sure, the flute, that's right!

(New music is heard, a high, rollicking tune.)

BEN. Father was a very great and a very wild-hearted
man. We would start in Boston, and he'd toss the
whole family into the wagon, and then he'd drive the
team right across the country; through Ohio, and
Indiana, Michigan, Illinois, and all the Western
states. And we'd stop in the towns and sell the flutes
that he'd made on the way. Great inventor, Father.
With one gadget he made more in a week than a man
like you could make in a lifetime.

WILLY. That's just the way I'm bringing them up, Ben –
rugged, well liked, all-around.

---

1 **why, boys:** hier: nun, Jungens.
7 **Ketchikan:** Stadt in Alaska.
9 **stock:** Familie, Abstammung.
15 **rollicking:** ausgelassen.
17 **to toss:** werfen, schmeißen.
23 **gadget:** Gerät, Ding; Erfindung.
26 **rugged:** robust.

BEN. Yeah? *(To Biff.)* Hit that, boy – hard as you can.
(He pounds his stomach.)

BIFF. Oh, no, sir!

BEN *(taking boxing stance)*. Come on, get to me! *(He
laughs.)*

WILLY. Go to it, Biff! Go ahead, show him!

BIFF. Okay! *(He cocks his fists and starts in.)*

LINDA *(to Willy)*. Why must he fight, dear?

BEN *(sparring with Biff)*. Good boy! Good boy!

WILLY. How's that, Ben, heh?

HAPPY. Give him the left, Biff!

LINDA. Why are you fighting?

BEN. Good boy! *(Suddenly comes in, trips Biff, and
stands over him, the point of his umbrella poised over
Biff's eye.)*

LINDA. Look out, Biff!

BIFF. Gee!

BEN *(patting Biff's knee)*. Never fight fair with a
stranger, boy. You'll never get out of the jungle that
way. *(Taking Linda's hand and bowing.)* It was an
honor and a pleasure to meet you, Linda.

LINDA *(withdrawing her hand coldly, frightened)*. Have a
nice – trip.

BEN *(to Willy)*. And good luck with your – what do you
do?

WILLY. Selling.

BEN. Yes. Well . . . *(He raises his hand in farewell to all.)*

---

2 **to pound:** schlagen auf.
4 **boxing stance:** Boxhaltung.
7 **to cock one's fists:** die Fäuste ballen.
9 **to spar:** sparren, Boxbewegungen machen.
13 **to trip s.o.:** jdn. zu Fall bringen.
14 **poised:** hier: schwebend gehalten.

WILLY. No, Ben, I don't want you to think . . . *(He takes Ben's arm to show him.)* It's Brooklyn, I know, but we hunt too.

BEN. Really, now.

5 WILLY. Oh, sure, there's snakes and rabbits and – that's why I moved out here. Why, Biff can fell any one of these trees in no time! Boys! Go right over to where they're building the apartment house and get some sand. We're gonna rebuild the entire front stoop
10 right now! Watch this, Ben!

BIFF. Yes, sir! On the double, Hap!

HAPPY *(as he and Biff run off)*. I lost weight, Pop, you notice?

*(Charley enters in knickers, even before the boys are
15 gone.)*

CHARLEY. Listen, if they steal any more from that building the watchman'll put the cops on them!

LINDA *(to Willy)*. Don't let Biff . . .

(Ben laughs lustily.)

20 WILLY. You shoulda seen the lumber they brought home last week. At least a dozen six-by-tens worth all kinds a money.

CHARLEY. Listen, if that watchman –

WILLY. I gave them hell, understand. But I got a couple
25 of fearless characters there.

CHARLEY. Willy, the jails are full of fearless characters.

---

6 **to fell:** fällen.
9 **stoop** (AE): Veranda.
17 **to put the cops on s.o.:** die Polizei auf jdn. hetzen.
19 **lustily** (adv.): lebhaft, derb.
20 **lumber** (AE): Bauholz.
21 **six-by-tens:** Balken mit den Maßen 6 *inch* zu 10 *inch*.

BEN *(clapping Willy on the back, with a laugh at Charley)*. And the stock exchange, friend!

WILLY *(joining in Ben's laughter)*. Where are the rest of your pants?

5 CHARLEY. My wife bought them.

WILLY. Now all you need is a golf club and you can go upstairs and go to sleep. *(To Ben.)* Great athlete! Between him and his son Bernard they can't hammer a nail!

10 BERNARD *(rushing in)*. The watchman's chasing Biff!

WILLY *(angrily)*. Shut up! He's not stealing anything!

LINDA *(alarmed, hurrying off left)*. Where is he? Biff, dear! *(She exits.)*

WILLY *(moving toward the left, away from Ben)*. There's
15 nothing wrong. What's the matter with you?

BEN. Nervy boy. Good!

WILLY *(laughing)*. Oh, nerves of iron, that Biff!

CHARLEY. Don't know what it is. My New England man comes back and he's bleedin', they murdered him up
20 there.

WILLY. It's contacts, Charley, I got important contacts!

CHARLEY *(sarcastically)*. Glad to hear it, Willy. Come in later, we'll shoot a little casino. I'll take some of your Portland money. *(He laughs at Willy and exits.)*

25 WILLY *(turning to Ben)*. Business is bad, it's murderous. But not for me, of course.

BEN. I'll stop by on my way back to Africa.

WILLY *(longingly)*. Can't you stay a few days? You're

---

2 **stock exchange:** Börse.
4 **pants** (pl.): Hose.
6 **golf club:** Golfschläger.
16 **nervy:** dreist, kaltblütig.
23 **casino:** Kartenspiel.
28 **longingly** (adv.): sehnsüchtig, sehnlich.

just what I need, Ben, because I – I have a fine
position here, but I – well, Dad left when I was such a
baby and I never had a chance to talk to him and I
still feel – kind of temporary about myself.

5 BEN. I'll be late for my train.

(They are at opposite ends of the stage.)

WILLY. Ben, my boys – can't we talk? They'd go into the
jaws of hell for me, see, but I –

BEN. William, you're being first-rate with your boys.
10 Outstanding, manly chaps!

WILLY *(hanging on to his words)*. Oh, Ben, that's good
to hear! Because sometimes I'm afraid that I'm not
teaching them the right kind of – Ben, how should I
teach them?

15 BEN *(giving great weight to each word, and with a certain
vicious audacity)*. William, when I walked into the
jungle, I was seventeen. When I walked out I was
twenty-one. And, by God, I was rich! *(He goes off
into darkness around the right corner of the house.)*

20 WILLY. ... was rich! That's just the spirit I want to imbue them with! To walk into a jungle! I was right! I
was right! I was right!

*(Ben is gone, but Willy is still speaking to him as
Linda, in nightgown and robe, enters the kitchen,
25 glances around for Willy, then goes to the door of the*

---

4 **temporary:** provisorisch; unfertig.
7 f. **to go into the jaws of hell:** durchs Feuer gehen.
9 **first-rate:** hier: große Klasse.
10 **chap** (coll.): Bursche.
16 **vicious:** bösartig.
   audacity: Unverfrorenheit, Frechheit.
20 f. **to imbue s.o. with s.th.:** jdn. mit etwas erfüllen.
24 **nightgown:** Nachthemd.

house, looks out and sees him. Comes down to his left.
He looks at her.)

LINDA. Willy, dear? Willy?

WILLY. I was right!

5 LINDA. Did you have some cheese? *(He can't answer.)*
It's very late, darling. Come to bed, heh?

WILLY *(looking straight up).* Gotta break your neck to
see a star in this yard.

LINDA. You coming in?

10 WILLY. Whatever happened to that diamond watch fob?
Remember? When Ben came from Africa that time?
Didn't he give me a watch fob with a diamond in it?

LINDA. You pawned it, dear. Twelve, thirteen years ago.
For Biff's radio correspondence course.

15 WILLY. Gee, that was a beautiful thing. I'll take a walk.

LINDA. But you're in your slippers.

WILLY *(starting to go around the house at the left).* I was
right! I was! *(Half to Linda, as he goes, shaking his
head.)* What a man! There was a man worth talking

20 to. I was right!

LINDA *(calling after Willy).* But in your slippers, Willy!
*(Willy is almost gone when Biff, in his pajamas, comes
down the stairs and enters the kitchen.)*

BIFF. What is he doing out there?

25 LINDA. Sh!

BIFF. God Almighty, Mom, how long has he been doing
this?

LINDA. Don't, he'll hear you.

BIFF. What the hell is the matter with him?

30 LINDA. It'll pass by morning.

---

10 **watch fob:** Anhänger für Uhrkette.
13 **to pawn:** verpfänden.

BIFF. Shouldn't we do anything?

LINDA. Oh, my dear, you should do a lot of things, but there's nothing to do, so go to sleep.

(Happy comes down the stair and sits on the steps.)

5 HAPPY. I never heard him so loud, Mom.

LINDA. Well, come around more often; you'll hear him. *(She sits down at the table and mends the lining of Willy's jacket.)*

BIFF. Why didn't you ever write me about this, Mom?

10 LINDA. How would I write to you? For over three months you had no address.

BIFF. I was on the move. But you know I thought of you all the time. You know that, don't you, pal?

LINDA. I know, dear, I know. But he likes to have a

15 letter. Just to know that there's still a possibility for better things.

BIFF. He's not like this all the time, is he?

LINDA. It's when you come home he's always the worst.

BIFF. When I come home?

20 LINDA. When you write you're coming, he's all smiles, and talks about the future, and – he's just wonderful. And then the closer you seem to come, the more shaky he gets, and then, by the time you get here, he's arguing, and he seems angry at you. I think it's

25 just that maybe he can't bring himself to – to open up to you. Why are you so hateful to each other? Why is that?

BIFF *(evasively)*. I'm not hateful, Mom.

LINDA. But you no sooner come in the door than you're

30 fighting!

---

7 **lining:** Futter (des Jacketts).

20 **to be all smiles:** heiter, fröhlich sein.

28 **evasively** (adv.): ausweichend.

BIFF. I don't know why. I mean to change. I'm tryin', Mom, you understand?

LINDA. Are you home to stay now?

BIFF. I don't know. I want to look around, see what's doin'.

LINDA. Biff, you can't look around all your life, can you?

BIFF. I just can't take hold, Mom. I can't take hold of some kind of a life.

LINDA. Biff, a man is not a bird, to come and go with the spring-time.

BIFF. Your hair ... *(He touches her hair.)* Your hair got so gray.

LINDA. Oh, it's been grey since you were in high school. I just stopped dyeing it, that's all.

BIFF. Dye it again, will ya? I don't want my pal looking old. *(He smiles.)*

LINDA. You're such a boy! You think you can go away for a year and ... You've got to get it into your head now that one day you'll knock on this door and there'll be strange people here –

BIFF. What are you talking about? You're not even sixty, Mom.

LINDA. But what about your father?

BIFF *(lamely)*. Well, I meant him too.

HAPPY. He admires Pop.

LINDA. Biff, dear, if you don't have any feeling for him, then you can't have any feeling for me.

BIFF. Sure I can, Mom.

LINDA. No. You can't just come to see me, because I

4f. **see what's doing:** mal sehen, was sich tut.

7 **to take hold of s.th.:** etwas festhalten; sich an etwas binden.

14 **to dye:** färben.

love him. *(With a threat, but only a threat, of tears.)*
He's the dearest man in the world to me, and I won't
have anyone making him feel unwanted and low and
blue. You've got to make up your mind now, darling,
5   there's no leeway any more. Either he's your father
and you pay him that respect, or else you're not to
come here. I know he's not easy to get along with –
nobody knows that better than me – but ...

WILLY *(from the left, with a laugh)*. Hey, hey, Biffo!
10 BIFF *(starting to go out after Willy)*. What the hell is the
matter with him? *(Happy stops him.)*

LINDA. Don't – don't go near him!

BIFF. Stop making excuses for him! He always, always
wiped the floor with you. Never had an ounce of
15 respect for you.

HAPPY. He's always had respect for –

BIFF. What the hell do you know about it?

HAPPY *(surlily)*. Just don't call him crazy!

BIFF. He's got no character – Charley wouldn't do this.
20 Not in his own house – spewing out that vomit from
his mind.

HAPPY. Charley never had to cope with what he's got to.

BIFF. People are worse off than Willy Loman. Believe
me, I've seen them!

---

3 **low:** hier: niedergeschlagen.
4 **blue:** schwermütig.
5 **there's no leeway:** es gibt keinen Spielraum mehr.
14 **to wipe the floor with s.o.:** (fig.) jdn. rücksichtslos behandeln.
18 **surlily** (adv.): mürrisch, finster.
20f. **to spew out the vomit from one's mind:** sich die Seele aus dem
Leib kotzen.
22 **to cope with s.th.:** mit etwas kämpfen; fertig werden mit etwas.
23 **to be worse off:** schlechter dran sein.

LINDA. Then make Charley your father, Biff. You can't
do that, can you? I don't say he's a great man. Willy
Loman never made a lot of money. His name was
never in the paper. He's not the finest character that
5 ever lived. But he's a human being, and a terrible
thing is happening to him. So attention must be paid.
He's not to be allowed to fall into his grave like an old
dog. Attention, attention must be finally paid to such
a person. You called him crazy –

10 BIFF. I didn't mean –

LINDA. No, a lot of people think he's lost his – balance.
But you don't have to be very smart to know what his
trouble is. The man is exhausted.

HAPPY. Sure!

15 LINDA. A small man can be just as exhausted as a great
man. He works for a company thirty-six years this
March, opens up unheard-of territories to their
trademark, and now in his old age they take his salary
away.

20 HAPPY *(indignantly)*. I didn't know that, Mom.

LINDA. You never asked, my dear! Now that you get
your spending money someplace else you don't trouble your mind with him.

HAPPY. But I gave you money last –

25 LINDA. Christmas time, fifty dollars! To fix the hot water
it cost ninety-seven fifty! For five weeks he's been on
straight commission, like a beginner, an unknown!

BIFF. Those ungrateful bastards!

LINDA. Are they any worse than his sons? When he

---

17 **unheard-of:** unbekannt; unerhört.
25 **to fix:** hier: in Ordnung bringen, reparieren (AE).
26 f. **to be on straight commission:** nur noch auf Provisionsbasis arbeiten.

brought them business, when he was young, they
were glad to see him. But now his old friends, the old
buyers that loved him so and always found some
order to hand him in a pinch – they're all dead, re-
tired. He used to be able to make six, seven calls a day
in Boston. Now he takes his valises out of the car and
puts them back and takes them out again and he's exhausted. Instead of walking he talks now. He drives
seven hundred miles, and when he gets there no one
knows him any more, no one welcomes him. And
what goes through a man's mind, driving seven hundred miles home without having earned a cent? Why
shouldn't he talk to himself? Why? When he has to go
to Charley and borrow fifty dollars a week and pre-
tend to me that it's his pay? How long can that go on?
How long? You see what I'm sitting here and waiting
for? And you tell me he has no character? The man
who never worked a day but for your benefit? When
does he get the medal for that? Is this his reward – to
turn around at the age of sixty-three and find his sons,
who he loved better than his life, one a philandering
bum –

HAPPY. Mom!

LINDA. That's all you are, my baby! *(To Biff.)* And you!
What happened to the love you had for him? You
were such pals! How you used to talk to him on the
phone every night! How lonely he was till he could
come home to you!

BIFF. All right, Mom. I'll live here in my room, and I'll
get a job. I'll keep away from him, that's all.

---

4 **in a pinch:** in einer Notlage, Zwickmühle.
21 **to philander:** herumflirten; sich als Schürzenjäger aufführen.

LINDA. No, Biff. You can't stay here and fight all the
    time.

BIFF. He threw me out of this house, remember that.

LINDA. Why did he do that? I never knew why.

5 BIFF. Because I know he's a fake and he doesn't like
    anybody around who knows!

LINDA. Why a fake? In what way? What do you mean?

BIFF. Just don't lay it all at my feet. It's between me and
    him – that's all I have to say. I'll chip in from now on.

10   He'll settle for half my pay check. He'll be all right.
    I'm going to bed. *(He starts for the stairs.)*

LINDA. He won't be all right.

BIFF *(turning on the stairs, furiously)*. I hate this city and
    I'll stay here. Now what do you want?

15 LINDA. He's dying, Biff.

    (Happy turns quickly to her, shocked.)

BIFF *(after a pause)*. Why is he dying?

LINDA. He's been trying to kill himself.

BIFF *(with great horror)*. How?

20 LINDA. I live from day to day.

BIFF. What're you talking about?

LINDA. Remember I wrote you that he smashed up the
    car again? In February?

BIFF. Well?

25 LINDA. The insurance inspector came. He said that they
    have evidence. That all these accidents in the last
    year – weren't – weren't – accidents.

HAPPY. How can they tell that? That's a lie.

---

  5 **fake:** Betrüger, Heuchler.

  8 **don't lay it all at my feet:** schieb nicht alles mir in die Schuhe.

  9 **to chip in:** (mit Geld oder Hilfe) einspringen.

10 **pay check** (AE): Gehalt; Gehaltsscheck.

LINDA. It seems there's a woman ... *(She takes a breath as)*

$\begin{cases} \text{BIFF } \textit{(sharply but contained).} \text{ What woman?} \\ \text{LINDA } \textit{(simultaneously).} \text{ ... and this woman ...} \end{cases}$

5 LINDA. What?

BIFF. Nothing. Go ahead.

LINDA. What did you say?

BIFF. Nothing. I just said what woman?

HAPPY. What about her?

10 LINDA. Well, it seems she was walking down the road and saw his car. She says that he wasn't driving fast at all, and that he didn't skid. She says he came to that little bridge, and then deliberately smashed into the railing, and it was only the shallowness of the water

15 that saved him.

BIFF. Oh, no, he probably just fell asleep again.

LINDA. I don't think he fell asleep.

BIFF. Why not?

LINDA. Last month ... *(With great difficulty.)* Oh, boys,

20 it's so hard to say a thing like this! He's just a big stupid man to you, but I tell you there's more good in him than in many other people. *(She chokes, wipes her eyes.)* I was looking for a fuse. The lights blew out, and I went down the cellar. And behind the fuse

25 box – it happened to fall out – was a length of rubber pipe – just short.

HAPPY. No kidding?

---

3 **contained:** beherrscht.
12 **to skid:** schleudern, rutschen.
22 **to choke:** hier: einen Weinanfall unterdrücken.
23 **fuse:** (elektrische) Sicherung.
25 f. **rubber pipe:** hier: Gasleitungsschlauch.

LINDA. There's a little attachment on the end of it. I knew right away. And sure enough, on the bottom of the water heater there's a new little nipple on the gas pipe.

5 HAPPY *(angrily)*. That – jerk.

BIFF. Did you have it taken off?

LINDA. I'm – I'm ashamed to. How can I mention it to him? Every day I go down and take away that little rubber pipe. But, when he comes home, I put it back

10 where it was. How can I insult him that way? I don't know what to do. I live from day to day, boys. I tell you, I know every thought in his mind. It sounds so old-fashioned and silly, but I tell you he put his whole life into you and you've turned your backs on him.

15 *(She is bent over in the chair, weeping, her face in her hands.)* Biff, I swear to God! Biff, his life is in your hands!

HAPPY *(to Biff)*. How do you like that damned fool!

BIFF *(kissing her)*. All right, pal, all right. It's all settled

20 now. I've been remiss. I know that, Mom. But now I'll stay, and I swear to you, I'll apply myself. *(Kneeling in front of her, in a fever of self-reproach.)* It's just – you see, Mom, I don't fit in business. Not that I won't try. I'll try, and I'll make good.

25 HAPPY. Sure you will. The trouble with you in business was you never tried to please people.

BIFF. I know, I –

HAPPY. Like when you worked for Harrison's. Bob Harrison said you were tops, and then you go and do

---

1 **attachment:** Verbindungsteil.

5 **jerk** (slang): mieser Kerl.

20 **remiss:** nachlässig, unaufmerksam, faul.

some damn fool thing like whistling whole songs in
the elevator like a comedian.

BIFF *(against Happy)*. So what? I like to whistle sometimes.

5 HAPPY. You don't raise a guy to a responsible job who
whistles in the elevator!

LINDA. Well, don't argue about it now.

HAPPY. Like when you'd go off and swim in the middle
of the day instead of taking the line around.

10 BIFF *(his resentment rising)*. Well, don't you run off?
You take off sometimes, don't you? On a nice summer day?

HAPPY. Yeah, but I cover myself!

LINDA. Boys!

15 HAPPY. If I'm going to take a fade the boss can call any
number where I'm supposed to be and they'll swear
to him that I just left. I'll tell you something that I
hate to say, Biff, but in the business world some of
them think you're crazy.

20 BIFF *(angered)*. Screw the business world!

HAPPY. All right, screw it! Great, but cover yourself!

LINDA. Hap, Hap!

BIFF. I don't care what they think! They've laughed at
Dad for years, and you know why? Because we don't

25 belong in this nuthouse of a city! We should be
mixing cement on some open plain, or – or carpen-
ters. A carpenter is allowed to whistle!

---

2 **elevator** (AE): Fahrstuhl, Aufzug.
  comedian: Komiker.
10 **resentment:** Groll.
15 **to take a fade** (slang): verschwinden; blau machen.
20 **to screw s.th.** (vulg.): auf etwas pfeifen.
25 **nuthouse:** Irrenhaus.

(*Willy walks in from the entrance of the house, at left.*)

WILLY. Even your grandfather was better than a carpenter. (*Pause. They watch him.*) You never grew up.
5   Bernard does not whistle in the elevator, I assure you.

BIFF (*as though to laugh Willy out of it*). Yeah, but you do, Pop.

WILLY. I never in my life whistled in an elevator! And
10   who in the business world thinks I'm crazy?

BIFF. I didn't mean it like that, Pop. Now don't make a whole thing out of it, will ya?

WILLY. Go back to the West! Be a carpenter, a cowboy, enjoy yourself!

15   LINDA. Willy, he was just saying –

WILLY. I heard what he said!

HAPPY (*trying to quiet Willy*). Hey, Pop, come on now . . .

WILLY (*continuing over Happy's line*). They laugh at me,
20   heh? Go to Filene's, go to the Hub, go to Slattery's, Boston. Call out the name Willy Loman and see what happens! Big shot!

BIFF. All right, Pop.

WILLY. Big!

25   BIFF. All right!

WILLY. Why do you always insult me?

BIFF. I didn't say a word. (*To Linda.*) Did I say a word?

LINDA. He didn't say anything, Willy.

WILLY (*going to the doorway of the living-room*). All
30   right, good night, good night.

LINDA. Willy, dear, he just decided . . .

---

22 **big shot** (coll.): großes Tier; hier: Verkaufskanone.

WILLY *(to Biff)*. If you get tired hanging around tomorrow, paint the ceiling I put up in the living-room.

BIFF. I'm leaving early tomorrow.

HAPPY. He's going to see Bill Oliver, Pop.

5 WILLY *(interestedly)*. Oliver? For what?

BIFF *(with reserve, but trying, trying)*. He always said he'd stake me. I'd like to go into business, so maybe I can take him up on it.

LINDA. Isn't that wonderful?

10 WILLY. Don't interrupt. What's wonderful about it? There's fifty men in the City of New York who'd stake him. *(To Biff.)* Sporting goods?

BIFF. I guess so. I know something about it and –

WILLY. He knows something about it! You know sport-
15 ing goods better than Spalding, for God's sake! How much is he giving you?

BIFF. I don't know, I didn't even see him yet, but –

WILLY. Then what're you talkin' about?

BIFF *(getting angry)*. Well, all I said was I'm gonna see
20 him, that's all!

WILLY *(turning away)*. Ah, you're counting your chickens again.

BIFF *(starting left for the stairs)*. Oh, Jesus, I'm going to sleep!

25 WILLY *(calling after him)*. Don't curse in this house!

BIFF *(turning)*. Since when did you get so clean?

HAPPY *(trying to stop them)*. Wait a . . .

WILLY. Don't use that language to me! I won't have it!

---

7 **to stake s.o.** (slang): jdm. unter die Arme greifen; jdn. unterstützen.
8 **to take s.o. up on s.th.:** jdn. beim Wort nehmen.
21 f. **to count one's chickens** *(before they are hatched)*: (fig.) das Fell des Bären verkaufen (ehe man ihn hat).

HAPPY *(grabbing Biff, shouts)*. Wait a minute! I got an
idea. I got a feasible idea. Come here, Biff, let's talk
this over now, let's talk some sense here. When I was
down in Florida last time, I thought of a great idea to
5 sell sporting goods. It just came back to me. You and
I, Biff – we have a line, the Loman Line. We train a
couple of weeks, and put on a couple of exhibitions,
see?

WILLY. That's an idea!

10 HAPPY. Wait! We form two basketball teams, see? Two
water-polo teams. We play each other. It's a million
dollars' worth of publicity. Two brothers, see? The
Loman Brothers. Displays in the Royal Palms – all
the hotels. And banners over the ring and the basket-
15 ball court: "Loman Brothers." Baby, we could sell
sporting goods!

WILLY. That is a one-million-dollar idea!

LINDA. Marvelous!

BIFF. I'm in great shape as far as that's concerned.

20 HAPPY. And the beauty of it is, Biff, it wouldn't be like a
business. We'd be out playin' ball again . . .

BIFF *(enthused)*. Yeah, that's . . .

WILLY. Million-dollar . . .

HAPPY. And you wouldn't get fed up with it, Biff. It'd be
25 the family again. There'd be the old honor, and
comradeship, and if you wanted to go off for a swim

---

2 **feasible:** durchführbar, machbar.
11 **water-polo:** Wasserball.
12 **publicity:** Reklame.
13 **display:** Ausstellung.
24 **to get fed up with s.th.:** von etwas genug haben; die Nase voll haben.
26 **comradeship:** Kameradschaft.

or somethin' – well, you'd do it! Without some smart
    cooky gettin' up ahead of you!

WILLY. Lick the world! You guys together could abso-
    lutely lick the civilized world.

5 BIFF. I'll see Oliver tomorrow. Hap, if we could work
    that out . . .

LINDA. Maybe things are beginning to –

WILLY *(wildly enthused, to Linda)*. Stop interrupting!
    (To Biff.) But don't wear sport jacket and slacks
10   when you see Oliver.

BIFF. No, I'll –

WILLY. A business suit, and talk as little as possible, and
    don't crack any jokes.

BIFF. He did like me. Always liked me.

15 LINDA. He loved you!

WILLY *(to Linda)*. Will you stop! *(To Biff.)* Walk in very
    serious. You are not applying for a boy's job. Money
    is to pass. Be quiet, fine, and serious. Everybody
    likes a kidder, but nobody lends him money.

20 HAPPY. I'll try to get some myself, Biff. I'm sure I can.

WILLY. I see great things for you kids, I think your
    troubles are over. But remember, start big and you'll
    end big. Ask for fifteen. How much you gonna ask
    for?

25 BIFF. Gee, I don't know –

WILLY. And don't say "Gee." "Gee" is a boy's word. A
    man walking in for fifteen thousand dollars does not
    say "Gee!"

1f. **smart cooky** (coll.): Schlaumeier.
3 **to lick s.o.** (coll.): jdn. besiegen, übertrumpfen.
9 **slacks** (pl.): sportliche Hose.
13 **to crack jokes**: Witze reißen.

BIFF. Ten, I think, would be top though.

WILLY. Don't be so modest. You always started too low.
Walk in with a big laugh. Don't look worried. Start
off with a couple of your good stories to lighten things
5   up. It's not what you say, it's how you say it – because
personality always wins the day.

LINDA. Oliver always thought the highest of him –

WILLY. Will you let me talk?

BIFF. Don't yell at her, Pop, will ya?

10 WILLY *(angrily)*. I was talking, wasn't I?

BIFF. I don't like you yelling at her all the time, and I'm
tellin' you, that's all.

WILLY. What're you, takin' over this house?

LINDA. Willy –

15 WILLY *(turning on her)*. Don't take his side all the time,
goddammit!

BIFF *(furiously)*. Stop yelling at her!

WILLY *(suddenly pulling on his cheek, beaten down, guilt
ridden)*. Give my best to Bill Oliver – he may
20   remember me. *(He exits through the living-room
doorway.)*

LINDA *(her voice subdued)*. What'd you have to start
that for? *(Biff turns away.)* You see how sweet he was
as soon as you talked hopefully? *(She goes over to
25   Biff.)* Come up and say good night to him. Don't let
him go to bed that way.

HAPPY. Come on, Biff, let's buck him up.

LINDA. Please, dear. Just say good night. It takes so little
to make him happy. Come. *(She goes through the*

18f. **guilt ridden:** schuldbewußt.
22 **subdued:** unterdrückt; leise, gedämpft.
27 **to buck s.o. up** (coll.): jdn. aufmuntern.

*living-room doorway, calling upstairs from within
the living-room).* Your pajamas are hanging in the
bathroom, Willy!

HAPPY *(looking toward where Linda went out).* What a
woman! They broke the mold when they made her.
You know that, Biff?

BIFF. He's off salary. My God, working on commission!

HAPPY. Well, let's face it: he's no hot-shot selling man.
Except that sometimes, you have to admit, he's a
sweet personality.

BIFF *(deciding).* Lend me ten bucks, will ya? I want to
buy some new ties.

HAPPY. I'll take you to a place I know. Beautiful stuff.
Wear one of my striped shirts tomorrow.

BIFF. She got gray. Mom got awful old. Gee, I'm gonna
go in to Oliver tomorrow and knock him for a –

HAPPY. Come on up. Tell that to Dad. Let's give him a
whirl. Come on.

BIFF *(steamed up).* You know, with ten thousand bucks,
boy!

HAPPY *(as they go into the living-room).* That's the talk,
Biff, that's the first time I've heard the old confidence
out of you! *(From within the living-room, fading off.)*
You're gonna live with me, kid, and any babe you
want just say the word . . . *(The last lines are hardly
heard. They are mounting the stairs to their parents'
bedroom.)*

---

5 **they broke the mold when they made her:** Redensart, etwa: So eine
Frau gibt es nicht ein zweites Mal (*mold:* Gieß-, Gußform).
8 **hot-shot selling man:** Verkaufskanone.
11 **buck** (slang): Dollar.
16 **to knock s.o. for s.th.:** jdn. anzapfen.
17f. **to give s.o. a whirl** (coll.): jdn. aufmöbeln.
19 **steamed up:** in Erregung, unter Volldampf.

LINDA *(entering her bedroom and addressing Willy, who is in the bathroom. She is straightening the bed for him)*. Can you do anything about the shower? It drips.

5 WILLY *(from the bathroom)*. All of a sudden everything falls to pieces! Goddam plumbing, oughta be sued, those people. I hardly finished putting it in and the thing ... *(His words rumble off.)*

LINDA. I'm just wondering if Oliver will remember him.
10   You think he might?

WILLY *(coming out of the bathroom in his pajamas)*. Remember him? What's the matter with you, you crazy? If he'd've stayed with Oliver he'd be on top by now! Wait'll Oliver gets a look at him. You don't
15   know the average caliber any more. The average young man today – *(he is getting into bed)* – is got a caliber of zero. Greatest thing in the world for him was to bum around.

(Biff and Happy enter the bedroom. Slight pause.)

20 WILLY *(stops short, looking at Biff)*. Glad to hear it, boy.

HAPPY. He wanted to say good night to you, sport.

WILLY *(to Biff)*. Yeah. Knock him dead, boy. What'd you want to tell me?

BIFF. Just take it easy, Pop. Good night. *(He turns to go.)*
25 WILLY *(unable to resist)*. And if anything falls off the desk while you're talking to him – like a package or something – don't you pick it up. They have office boys for that.

---

6 **plumbing:** hier: Wasserleitungen.
  to sue s.o.: jdn. verklagen.
8 **to rumble off:** grollend verklingen.
18 **to bum around:** sich herumtreiben.
21 **sport** (coll.): Sportsfreund (Anrede).

LINDA. I'll make a big breakfast –

WILLY. Will you let me finish? *(To Biff.)* Tell him you were in the business in the West. Not farm work.

BIFF. All right, Dad.

5 LINDA. I think everything –

WILLY *(going right through her speech)*. And don't undersell yourself. No less than fifteen thousand dollars.

BIFF *(unable to bear him)*. Okay. Good night, Mom. *(He*
10 *starts moving.)*

WILLY. Because you got a greatness in you, Biff, remember that. You got all kinds a greatness . . . *(He lies back, exhausted. Biff walks out.)*

LINDA *(calling after Biff)*. Sleep well, darling!

15 HAPPY. I'm gonna get married, Mom. I wanted to tell you.

LINDA. Go to sleep, dear.

HAPPY *(going)*. I just wanted to tell you.

WILLY. Keep up the good work. *(Happy exits.)* God . . .
20 remember that Ebbets Field game? The championship of the city?

LINDA. Just rest. Should I sing to you?

WILLY. Yeah. Sing to me. *(Linda hums a soft lullaby.)* When that team came out – he was the tallest,
25 remember?

LINDA. Oh, yes. And in gold.

(Biff enters the darkened kitchen, takes a cigarette, and leaves the house. He comes downstage into a golden pool of light. He smokes, staring at the night.)

---

7 **to undersell o.s.:** sich unter Wert verkaufen.

19 **keep up the good work** (coll.): mach weiter so; bleib am Ball.

23 **lullaby:** Wiegenlied.

WILLY. Like a young god. Hercules – something like that. And the sun, the sun all around him. Remember how he waved to me? Right up from the field, with the representatives of three colleges standing by? And the buyers I brought, and the cheers when he came out – Loman, Loman, Loman! God Almighty, he'll be great yet. A star like that, magnificent, can never really fade away!

(The light on Willy is fading. The gas heater begins to glow through the kitchen wall, near the stairs, a blue flame beneath red coils.)

LINDA *(timidly)*. Willy dear, what has he got against you?

WILLY. I'm so tired. Don't talk any more.

(Biff slowly returns to the kitchen. He stops, stares toward the heater.)

LINDA. Will you ask Howard to let you work in New York?

WILLY. First thing in the morning. Everything'll be all right.

(Biff reaches behind the heater and draws out a length of rubber tubing. He is horrified and turns his head toward Willy's room, still dimly lit, from which the strains of Linda's desperate but monotonous humming rise.)

WILLY *(staring through the window into the moonlight)*. Gee, look at the moon moving between the buildings! *(Biff wraps the tubing around his hand and quickly goes up the stairs.)*

---

11 **coil:** Spirale; Heizschlange.
22 **horrified:** entsetzt.
24 **strains:** hier: Klänge.
   monotonous: eintönig.

Act Two

Music is heard, gay and bright. The curtain rises as the music fades away. Willy, in shirt sleeves, is sitting at the kitchen table, sipping coffee, his hat in his lap. Linda is filling his cup when she can.

WILLY. Wonderful coffee. Meal in itself.

LINDA. Can I make you some eggs?

WILLY. No. Take a breath.

LINDA. You look so rested, dear.

WILLY. I slept like a dead one. First time in months. Imagine, sleeping till ten on a Tuesday morning. Boys left nice and early, heh?

LINDA. They were out of here by eight o'clock.

WILLY. Good work!

LINDA. It was so thrilling to see them leaving together. I can't get over the shaving lotion in this house!

WILLY *(smiling)*. Mmm –

LINDA. Biff was very changed this morning. His whole attitude seemed to be hopeful. He couldn't wait to get downtown to see Oliver.

WILLY. He's heading for a change. There's no question, there simply are certain men that take longer to get – solidified. How did he dress?

LINDA. His blue suit. He's so handsome in that suit. He could be a – anything in that suit!

---

6 (a) **meal in itself:** eine Mahlzeit für sich.

23 **solidified:** gefestigt.

(Willy gets up from the table. Linda holds his jacket for him.)

WILLY. There's no question, no question at all. Gee, on the way home tonight I'd like to buy some seeds.

5 LINDA *(laughing)*. That'd be wonderful. But not enough sun gets back there. Nothing'll grow any more.

WILLY. You wait, kid, before it's all over we're gonna get a little place out in the country, and I'll raise some vegetables, a couple of chickens . . .

10 LINDA. You'll do it yet, dear.

(Willy walks out of his jacket. Linda follows him.)

WILLY. And they'll get married, and come for a weekend. I'd build a little guest house. 'Cause I got so many fine tools, all I'd need would be a little

15 lumber and some peace of mind.

LINDA *(joyfully)*. I sewed the lining . . .

WILLY. I could build two guest houses, so they'd both come. Did he decide how much he's going to ask Oliver for?

20 LINDA *(getting him into the jacket)*. He didn't mention it, but I imagine ten or fifteen thousand. You going to talk to Howard today?

WILLY. Yeah. I'll put it to him straight and simple. He'll just have to take me off the road.

25 LINDA. And Willy, don't forget to ask for a little advance, because we've got the insurance premium. It's the grace period now.

WILLY. That's a hundred . . .?

LINDA. A hundred and eight, sixty-eight. Because we're

30 a little short again.

---

25 f. **advance:** hier: Vorschuß.
26 **insurance premium:** Versicherungsprämie.
27 **grace period:** Aufschubfrist.

WILLY. Why are we short?

LINDA. Well, you had the motor job on the car . . .

WILLY. That goddam Studebaker!

LINDA. And you got one more payment on the
refrigerator . . .

WILLY. But it just broke again!

LINDA. Well, it's old, dear.

WILLY. I told you we should've bought a well-advertised
machine. Charley bought a General Electric and it's
twenty years old and it's still good, that son-of-a-
bitch.

LINDA. But, Willy –

WILLY. Whoever heard of a Hastings refrigerator? Once
in my life I would like to own something outright
before it's broken! I'm always in a race with the
junkyard! I just finished paying for the car and it's on
its last legs. The refrigerator consumes belts like a
goddam maniac. They time those things. They time
them so when you finally paid for them, they're used
up.

LINDA (*buttoning up his jacket as he unbuttons it*). All
told, about two hundred dollars would carry us, dear.
But that includes the last payment on the mortgage.
After this payment, Willy, the house belongs to us.

WILLY. It's twenty-five years!

---

4 **payment:** hier: Rate.

8f. **well-advertised machine:** hier: Markengerät.

14 **outright:** ganz und gar.

16 **junkyard:** Müllkippe, Schrotthaufen.

16f. **to be on one's last leg:** aus dem letzten Loch pfeifen.

18 **maniac:** Verrückter.

  to time s.th.: hier: etwas auf schnellen Verschleiß anlegen.

23 **mortgage:** Hypothek.

LINDA. Biff was nine years old when we bought it.

WILLY. Well, that's a great thing. To weather a twenty-five year mortgage is –

LINDA. It's an accomplishment.

5 WILLY. All the cement, the lumber, the reconstruction I put in this house! There ain't a crack to be found in it any more.

LINDA. Well, it served its purpose.

WILLY. What purpose? Some stranger'll come along,
10 move in, and that's that. If only Biff would take this house, and raise a family . . . *(He starts to go.)* Goodby, I'm late.

LINDA *(suddenly remembering).* Oh, I forgot! You're supposed to meet them for dinner.

15 WILLY. Me?

LINDA. At Frank's Chop House on Forty-eighth near Sixth Avenue.

WILLY. Is that so! How about you?

LINDA. No, just the three of you. They're gonna blow
20 you to a big meal!

WILLY. Don't say! Who thought of that?

LINDA. Biff came to me this morning, Willy, and he said, "Tell Dad, we want to blow him to a big meal." Be there six o'clock. You and your two boys are going to
25 have dinner.

WILLY. Gee whiz! That's really somethin'. I'm gonna knock Howard for a loop, kid. I'll get an advance,

---

2 **to weather** (coll.): hier: durchhalten, überstehen.
4 **accomplishment:** Leistung.
19 f. **they're gonna blow you to a big meal** (coll.): sie wollen dich zu einem verschwenderischen Essen einladen.
26 **gee whiz!** (coll.): Ausruf des Erstaunens.
27 **to knock s.o. for a loop:** jdn. beeindrucken; bei jdm. Erstaunen hervorrufen.

and I'll come home with a New York job. Goddammit, now I'm gonna do it!

LINDA. Oh, that's the spirit, Willy!

WILLY. I will never get behind a wheel the rest of my life!

5 LINDA. It's changing, Willy, I can feel it changing!

WILLY. Beyond a question. G'by, I'm late. *(He starts to
go again.)*

LINDA *(calling after him as she runs to the kitchen table
for a handkerchief)*. You got your glasses?

10 WILLY *(feels for them, then comes back in)*. Yeah, yeah,
got my glasses.

LINDA *(giving him the handkerchief)*. And a handkerchief.

WILLY. Yeah, handkerchief.

15 LINDA. And your saccharine?

WILLY. Yeah, my saccharine.

LINDA. Be careful on the subway stairs.

*(She kisses him, and a silk stocking is seen hanging
from her hand. Willy notices it.)*

20 WILLY. Will you stop mending stockings? At least while
I'm in the house. It gets me nervous. I can't tell you.
Please.

*(Linda hides the stocking in her hand as she follows
Willy across the forestage in front of the house.)*

25 LINDA. Remember, Frank's Chop House.

WILLY *(passing the apron)*. Maybe beets would grow out
there.

LINDA *(laughing)*. But you tried so many times.

WILLY. Yeah. Well, don't work hard today. *(He disap-
30 pears around the right corner of the house.)*

---

3 **that's the spirit** (coll.): das ist die richtige Gesinnung.
15 **saccharine:** Saccharin (Süßstoff).
26 **beets:** Rüben.

LINDA. Be careful!

(As Willy vanishes, Linda waves to him. Suddenly the phone rings. She runs across the stage and into the kitchen and lifts it.)

5 LINDA. Hello? Oh, Biff! I'm so glad you called, I just … Yes, sure, I just told him. Yes, he'll be there for dinner at six o'clock, I didn't forget. Listen, I was just dying to tell you. You know that little rubber pipe I told you about? That he connected to the gas heater?
10 I finally decided to go down the cellar this morning and take it away and destroy it. But it's gone! Imagine? He took it away himself, it isn't there! *(She listens.)* When? Oh, then you took it. Oh – nothing, it's just that I'd hoped he'd taken it away himself. Oh,
15 I'm not worried, darling, because this morning he left in such high spirits, it was like the old days! I'm not afraid any more. Did Mr. Oliver see you? … Well, you wait there then. And make a nice impression on him, darling. Just don't perspire too much before you
20 see him. And have a nice time with Dad. He may have big news too! … That's right, a New York job. And be sweet to him tonight, dear. Be loving to him. Because he's only a little boat looking for a harbor. *(She is trembling with sorrow and joy.)* Oh, that's
25 wonderful, Biff, you'll save his life. Thanks, darling. Just put your arm around him when he comes into the restaurant. Give him a smile. That's the boy … Good-by, dear. … You got your comb? … That's fine. Good-by, Biff dear.
30 *(In the middle of her speech, Howard Wagner, thirty-*

7f. **I am dying to tell you:** ich muß es dir unbedingt sagen.
19 **to perspire:** schwitzen, transpirieren.

*six, wheels on a small typewriter table on which is a
wire-recording machine and proceeds to plug it in.
This is on the left forestage. Light slowly fades on
Linda as it rises on Howard. Howard is intent on
5 threading the machine and only glances over his shoulder as Willy appears.)*

WILLY. Pst! Pst!

HOWARD. Hello, Willy, come in.

WILLY. Like to have a little talk with you, Howard.

10 HOWARD. Sorry to keep you waiting. I'll be with you in a
minute.

WILLY. What's that, Howard?

HOWARD. Didn't you ever see one of these? Wire
recorder.

15 WILLY. Oh. Can we talk a minute?

HOWARD. Records things. Just got delivery yesterday.
Been driving me crazy, the most terrific machine I
ever saw in my life. I was up all night with it.

WILLY. What do you do with it?

20 HOWARD. I bought it for dictation, but you can do
anything with it. Listen to this. I had it home last
night. Listen to what I picked up. The first one is my
daughter. Get this. *(He flicks the switch and "Roll out
the Barrel" is heard being whistled.)* Listen to that kid
25 whistle.

WILLY. That is lifelike, isn't it?

---

2 **wire-recording machine:** Drahttonaufnahmegerät (Vorläufer des
Tonbandgerätes; nahm auf einer Drahtspule statt auf einem Ma-
gnetband auf).
to plug in: in eine Steckdose einstöpseln.

4 **to be intent on s.th.:** eifrig bedacht sein auf etwas.

5 **to thread:** hier: einfädeln.

23 **to flick the switch:** den Schalter schnell umlegen.

HOWARD. Seven years old. Get that tone.

WILLY. Ts, ts. Like to ask a little favor if you ...
(The whistling breaks off, and the voice of Howard's daughter is heard.)

5 HIS DAUGHTER. "Now you, Daddy."

HOWARD. She's crazy for me! *(Again the same song is whistled.)* That's me! Ha! *(He winks.)*

WILLY. You're very good!
(The whistling breaks off again. The machine runs
10 *silent for a moment.)*

HOWARD. Sh! Get this now, this is my son.

HIS SON. "The capital of Alabama is Montgomery; the capital of Arizona is Phoenix; the capital of Arkansas is Little Rock; the capital of California is Sacra-
15 mento..." *(and on, and on.)*

HOWARD *(holding up five fingers).* Five years old, Willy!

WILLY. He'll make an announcer some day!

HIS SON *(continuing).* "The capital ..."

HOWARD. Get that – alphabetical order! *(The machine*
20 *breaks off suddenly.)* Wait a minute. The maid kicked the plug out.

WILLY. It certainly is a –

HOWARD. Sh, for God's sake!

HIS SON. "It's nine o'clock, Bulova watch time. So I have
25 to go to sleep."

WILLY. That really is –

HOWARD. Wait a minute! The next is my wife.
(They wait.)

HOWARD'S VOICE. "Go on, say something." *(Pause.)*
30 "Well, you gonna talk?"

---

7 **to wink at s.o.:** jdm. zuzwinkern.
17 **announcer:** Radiosprecher, -ansager.
21 **plug:** Stecker.

HIS WIFE. "I can't think of anything."

HOWARD'S VOICE. "Well, talk – it's turning."

HIS WIFE *(shyly, beaten)*. "Hello." *(Silence.)* "Oh, Howard, I can't talk into this ..."

5 HOWARD *(snapping the machine off)*. That was my wife.

WILLY. That is a wonderful machine. Can we –

HOWARD. I tell you, Willy, I'm gonna take my camera, and my bandsaw, and all my hobbies, and out they go. This is the most fascinating relaxation I ever

10 found.

WILLY. I think I'll get one myself.

HOWARD. Sure, they're only a hundred and a half. You can't do without it. Supposing you wanna hear Jack Benny, see? But you can't be at home at that hour.

15 So you tell the maid to turn the radio on when Jack Benny comes on, and this automatically goes on with the radio ...

WILLY. And when you come home you ...

HOWARD. You can come home twelve o'clock, one

20 o'clock, any time you like, and you get yourself a Coke and sit yourself down, throw the switch, and there's Jack Benny's program in the middle of the night!

WILLY. I'm definitely going to get one. Because lots of

25 time I'm on the road, and I think to myself, what I must be missing on the radio!

HOWARD. Don't you have a radio in the car?

WILLY. Well, yeah, but who ever thinks of turning it on?

---

5 **to snap off:** ausknipsen, abstellen.
8 **bandsaw:** Bandsäge.
9 **relaxation:** Entspannung, Erholung.
13 f. **Benny:** Jack B., berühmter amerikanischer Komiker.
21 **to throw the switch:** den Schalter umlegen.

HOWARD. Say, aren't you supposed to be in Boston?

WILLY. That's what I want to talk to you about, Howard.
You got a minute? *(He draws a chair in from the wing.)*

5 HOWARD. What happened? What're you doing here?

WILLY. Well ...

HOWARD. You didn't crack up again, did you?

WILLY. Oh, no. No ...

HOWARD. Geez, you had me worried there for a minute.
10   What's the trouble?

WILLY. Well, tell you the truth, Howard. I've come to
the decision that I'd rather not travel any more.

HOWARD. Not travel! Well, what'll you do?

WILLY. Remember, Christmas time, when you had the
15   party here? You said you'd try to think of some spot
for me here in town.

HOWARD. With us?

WILLY. Well, sure.

HOWARD. Oh, yeah, yeah. I remember. Well, I couldn't
20   think of anything for you, Willy.

WILLY. I tell ya, Howard. The kids are all grown up,
y'know. I don't need much any more. If I could take
home – well, sixty-five dollars a week, I could swing it.

HOWARD. Yeah, but Willy, see I –

25 WILLY. I tell ya why, Howard. Speaking frankly and
between the two of us, y'know – I'm just a little tired.

HOWARD. Oh, I could understand that, Willy. But you're
a road man, Willy, and we do a road business. We've
only got a half-dozen salesmen on the floor here.

---

4 **wing:** hier: Kulisse; Bühnenseite.
7 **to crack up:** körperlich oder seelisch zusammenbrechen.
23 **I could swing it** (coll.): dann könnte ich das Ding schaukeln; dann
käme ich hin.

WILLY. God knows, Howard, I never asked a favor of any man. But I was with the firm when your father used to carry you in here in his arms.

HOWARD. I know that, Willy, but –

5 WILLY. Your father came to me the day you were born and asked me what I thought of the name of Howard, may he rest in peace.

HOWARD. I appreciate that, Willy, but there just is no spot here for you. If I had a spot I'd slam you right in, 0 but I just don't have a single solitary spot.

(He looks for his lighter. Willy has picked it up and gives it to him. Pause.)

WILLY *(with increasing anger)*. Howard, all I need to set my table is fifty dollars a week.

15 HOWARD. But where am I going to put you, kid?

WILLY. Look, it isn't a question of whether I can sell merchandise, is it?

HOWARD. No, but it's a business, kid, and everybody's gotta pull his own weight.

20 WILLY *(desperately)*. Just let me tell you a story, Howard –

HOWARD. 'Cause you gotta admit, business is business.

WILLY *(angrily)*. Business is definitely business, but just listen for a minute. You don't understand this. When 25 I was a boy – eighteen, nineteen – I was already on the road. And there was a question in my mind as to whether selling had a future for me. Because in those days I had a yearning to go to Alaska. See, there were

---

9 **to slam:** hier: reinquetschen; eine Stelle geben.
13 f. **to set my table:** (fig.) mein Auskommen haben.
19 **to pull one's own weight:** (fig.) für sich selbst sorgen.
28 **yearning:** Verlangen; Sehnsucht.

three gold strikes in one month in Alaska, and I felt like going out. Just for the ride, you might say.

HOWARD *(barely interested).* Don't say.

WILLY. Oh, yeah, my father lived many years in Alaska.
5   He was an adventurous man. We've got quite a little streak of self-reliance in our family. I thought I'd go out with my older brother and try to locate him, and maybe settle in the North with the old man. And I was almost decided to go, when I met a salesman in
10 the Parker House. His name was Dave Singleman. And he was eighty-four years old, and he'd drummed merchandise in thirty-one states. And old Dave, he'd go up to his room, y'understand, put on his green velvet slippers – I'll never forget – and pick up his
15 phone and call the buyers, and without ever leaving his room, at the age of eighty-four, he made his living. And when I saw that, I realized that selling was the greatest career a man could want. 'Cause what could be more satisfying than to be able to go, at
20 the age of eighty-four, into twenty or thirty different cities, and pick up a phone, and be remembered and loved and helped by so many different people? Do you know? when he died – and by the way he died the death of a salesman, in his green velvet slippers in the
25 smoker of the New York, New Haven and Hartford, going into Boston – when he died, hundreds of salesmen and buyers were at his funeral. Things were sad

---

1 **gold strikes** (AE): Goldfunde.
6 **streak:** Spur, Anflug.
  self-reliance: Selbstvertrauen.
7 **to locate:** ausmachen, finden.
11f. **to drum merchandise** (AE, coll.): als Vertreter Ware verkaufen.
25 **smoker:** hier: Raucherabteil.

on a lotta trains for months after that. *(He stands up. Howard has not looked at him.)* In those days there was personality in it, Howard. There was respect, and comradeship, and gratitude in it. Today, it's all cut and dried, and there's no chance for bringing friendship to bear – or personality. You see what I mean? They don't know me any more.

HOWARD *(moving away, toward the right)*. That's just the thing, Willy.

WILLY. If I had forty dollars a week – that's all I'd need. Forty dollars, Howard.

HOWARD. Kid, I can't take blood from a stone, I –

WILLY *(desperation is on him now)*. Howard, the year Al Smith was nominated, your father came to me and –

HOWARD *(starting to go off)*. I've got to see some people, kid.

WILLY *(stopping him)*. I'm talking about your father! There were promises made across this desk! You mustn't tell me you've got people to see – I put thirty-four years into this firm, Howard, and now I can't pay my insurance! You can't eat the orange and throw the peel away – a man is not a piece of fruit! *(After a pause.)* Now pay attention. Your father – in 1928 I had a big year. I averaged a hundred and seventy dollars a week in commissions.

HOWARD *(impatiently)*. Now, Willy, you never averaged –

---

12 **I can't take blood from a stone:** Redensart, etwa: Ich kann's mir nicht aus den Rippen schneiden.
14 **Al Smith:** Alfred Emanuel S. (1873–1944), demokratischer Präsidentschaftskandidat 1928.
27 f. **to average:** hier: durchschnittlich verdienen.

WILLY *(banging his hand on the desk)*. I averaged a
hundred and seventy dollars a week in the year of
1928! And your father came to me – or rather, I was
in the office here – it was right over this desk – and he
5 put his hand on my shoulder –

HOWARD *(getting up)*. You'll have to excuse me, Willy, I
gotta see some people. Pull yourself together. *(Going
out.)* I'll be back in a little while.

*(On Howard's exit, the light on his chair grows very
10 bright and strange.)*

WILLY. Pull myself together! What the hell did I say to
him? My God, I was yelling at him! How could I!
*(Willy breaks off, staring at the light, which occupies
the chair, animating it. He approaches this chair,*
15 *standing across the desk from it.)* Frank, Frank, don't
you remember what you told me that time? How you
put your hand on my shoulder, and Frank ... *(He
leans on the desk and as he speaks the dead man's
name he accidentally switches on the recorder, and*
20 *instantly)*

HOWARD'S SON. "... of New York is Albany. The capital
of Ohio is Cincinnati, the capital of Rhode Island
is ..." *(The recitation continues.)*

WILLY *(leaping away with fright, shouting)*. Ha! How-
25 ard! Howard! Howard!

HOWARD *(rushing in)*. What happened?

WILLY *(pointing at the machine, which continues nasally,
childishly, with the capital cities)*. Shut it off! Shut it
off!

30 HOWARD *(pulling the plug out)*. Look, Willy ...

---

1 **to bang:** schlagen, knallen.
14 **to animate:** beleben; lebendig werden lassen.

WILLY *(pressing his hands to his eyes)*. I gotta get myself some coffee. I'll get some coffee . . .

(Willy starts to walk out. Howard stops him.)

HOWARD *(rolling up the cord)*. Willy, look . . .

5 WILLY. I'll go to Boston.

HOWARD. Willy, you can't go to Boston for us.

WILLY. Why can't I go?

HOWARD. I don't want you to represent us. I've been meaning to tell you for a long time now.

10 WILLY. Howard, are you firing me?

HOWARD. I think you need a good long rest, Willy.

WILLY. Howard –

HOWARD. And when you feel better, come back, and we'll see if we can work something out.

15 WILLY. But I gotta earn money, Howard. I'm in no position to –

HOWARD. Where are your sons? Why don't your sons give you a hand?

WILLY. They're working on a very big deal.

20 HOWARD. This is no time for false pride, Willy. You go to your sons and you tell them that you're tired. You've got two great boys, haven't you?

WILLY. Oh, no question, no question, but in the meantime . . .

25 HOWARD. Then that's that, heh?

WILLY. All right, I'll go to Boston tomorrow.

HOWARD. No, no.

WILLY. I can't throw myself on my sons. I'm not a cripple!

---

4 **cord:** Elektrokabel.

8f. **I've been meaning to tell you:** ich wollte dir schon lange sagen.

19 **big deal:** großes Geschäft, wichtige Sache.

28 **to throw o.s. on s.o.:** jdm. zur Last fallen.

HOWARD. Look, kid, I'm busy this morning.

WILLY *(grasping Howard's arm)*. Howard, you've got to
let me go to Boston!

HOWARD *(hard, keeping himself under control)*. I've got
5 a line of people to see this morning. Sit down, take
five minutes, and pull yourself together, and then go
home, will ya? I need the office, Willy. *(He starts to
go, turns, remembering the recorder, starts to push off
the table holding the recorder.)* Oh, yeah. Whenever
10 you can this week, stop by and drop off the samples.
You'll feel better, Willy, and then come back and
we'll talk. Pull yourself together, kid, there's people
outside.

(Howard exits, pushing the table off left. Willy stares
15 *into space, exhausted. Now the music is heard – Ben's*
music – first distantly, then closer, closer. As Willy
speaks, Ben enters from the right. He carries valise
and umbrella.)

WILLY. Oh, Ben, how did you do it? What is the answer?
20 Did you wind up the Alaska deal already?

BEN. Doesn't take much time if you know what you're
doing. Just a short business trip. Boarding ship in an
hour. Wanted to say good-by.

WILLY. Ben, I've got to talk to you.

25 BEN *(glancing at his watch)*. Haven't the time, William.

WILLY *(crossing the apron to Ben)*. Ben, nothing's working out. I don't know what to do.

BEN. Now, look here, William. I've bought timberland
in Alaska and I need a man to look after things for me.

---

10 **sample:** Muster, Probe.
20 **to wind up** (coll.): beenden; abwickeln.
22 **to board ship:** an Bord gehen.
28 **timberland:** hier: Wälder (zur Holzgewinnung).

WILLY. God, timberland! Me and my boys in those grand
outdoors!

BEN. You've a new continent at your doorstep, William.
Get out of these cities, they're full of talk and time
payments and courts of law. Screw on your fists and
you can fight for a fortune up there.

WILLY. Yes, yes! Linda, Linda!

(Linda enters as of old, with the wash.)

LINDA. Oh, you're back?

BEN. I haven't much time.

WILLY. No, wait! Linda, he's got a proposition for me in
Alaska.

LINDA. But you've got – *(To Ben.)* He's got a beautiful
job here.

WILLY. But in Alaska, kid, I could –

LINDA. You're doing well enough, Willy!

BEN *(to Linda)*. Enough for what, my dear?

LINDA *(frightened of Ben and angry at him)*. Don't say
those things to him! Enough to be happy right here,
right now. *(To Willy, while Ben laughs.)* Why must
everybody conquer the world? You're well liked, and
the boys love you, and someday – *(to Ben)* – why, old
man Wagner told him just the other day that if he
keeps it up he'll be a member of the firm, didn't he,
Willy?

WILLY. Sure, sure. I am building something with this
firm, Ben, and if a man is building something he must
be on the right track, mustn't he?

BEN. What are you building? Lay your hand on it.
Where is it?

WILLY *(hesitantly)*. That's true, Linda, there's nothing.

LINDA. Why? *(To Ben.)* There's a man eighty-four years
old –

WILLY. That's right, Ben, that's right. When I look at
that man I say, what is there to worry about?

BEN. Bah!

WILLY. It's true, Ben. All he has to do is go into any city,
5   pick up the phone, and he's making his living and you
know why?

BEN *(picking up his valise)*. I've got to go.

WILLY *(holding Ben back)*. Look at this boy!

(Biff, in his high school sweater, enters carrying suit-
10   *case. Happy carries Biff's shoulder guards, gold hel-*
met, and football pants.)

WILLY. Without a penny to his name, three great universities are begging for him, and from there the
sky's the limit, because it's not what you do, Ben.
15   It's who you know and the smile on your face! It's
contacts, Ben, contacts! The whole wealth of Alaska
passes over the lunch table at the Commodore Hotel,
and that's the wonder, the wonder of this country,
that a man can end with diamonds here on the basis
20   of being liked! *(He turns to Biff.)* And that's why
when you get out on that field today it's important.
Because thousands of people will be rooting for you
and loving you. *(To Ben, who has again begun to*
leave.) And Ben! when he walks into a business office
25   his name will sound out like a bell and all the doors
will open to him! I've seen it, Ben, I've seen it a
thousand times! You can't feel it with your hand like
timber, but it's there!

BEN. Good-by, William.

---

10 **shoulder guards:** Schulterpolster zum Schutz der Spieler.
12 **without a penny to his name:** ohne daß er einen Pfennig hat.
22 **to root for s.o.:** jdm. zujubeln.

WILLY. Ben, am I right? Don't you think I'm right? I
value your advice.

BEN. There's a new continent at your doorstep, William.
You could walk out rich. Rich! *(He is gone.)*

5 WILLY. We'll do it here, Ben! You hear me? We're
gonna do it here!
*(Young Bernard rushes in. The gay music of the Boys
is heard.)*

BERNARD. Oh, gee, I was afraid you left already!

0 WILLY. Why? What time is it?

BERNARD. It's half-past one!

WILLY. Well, come on, everybody! Ebbets Field next
stop! Where's the pennants? *(He rushes through the
wall-line of the kitchen and out into the living-room.)*

5 LINDA *(to Biff)*. Did you pack fresh underwear?

BIFF *(who has been limbering up)*. I want to go!

BERNARD. Biff, I'm carrying your helmet, ain't I?

HAPPY. No, I'm carrying the helmet.

BERNARD. Oh, Biff, you promised me.

0 HAPPY. I'm carrying the helmet.

BERNARD. How am I going to get in the locker room?

LINDA. Let him carry the shoulder guards. *(She puts her
coat and hat on in the kitchen.)*

BERNARD. Can I, Biff? 'Cause I told everybody I'm

5 going to be in the locker room.

HAPPY. In Ebbets Field it's the clubhouse.

BERNARD. I meant the clubhouse. Biff!

HAPPY. Biff!

BIFF *(grandly, after a slight pause)*. Let him carry the

0 shoulder guards.

---

13 **pennant:** Siegeszeichen; Wimpel.
16 **to limber up:** sich gelenkig machen; aufwärmen.
29 **grandly** (adv.): großzügig.

HAPPY *(as he gives Bernard the shoulder guards).* Stay
close to us now.

(Willy rushes in with the pennants.)

WILLY *(handing them out).* Everybody wave when Biff
comes out on the field. *(Happy and Bernard run off.)*
You set now, boy?

(The music has died away.)

BIFF. Ready to go, Pop. Every muscle is ready.

WILLY *(at the edge of the apron).* You realize what this
means?

BIFF. That's right, Pop.

WILLY *(feeling Biff's muscles).* You're comin' home this
afternoon captain of the All-Scholastic Championship Team of the City of New York.

BIFF. I got it, Pop. And remember, pal, when I take off
my helmet, that touchdown is for you.

WILLY. Let's go! *(He is starting out, with his arm around
Biff, when Charley enters, as of old, in knickers.)* I got
no room for you, Charley.

CHARLEY. Room? For what?

WILLY. In the car.

CHARLEY. You goin' for a ride? I wanted to shoot some
casino.

WILLY *(furiously).* Casino! *(Incredulously.)* Don't you
realize what today is?

LINDA. Oh, he knows, Willy. He's just kidding you.

WILLY. That's nothing to kid about!

CHARLEY. No, Linda, what's goin' on?

LINDA. He's playing in Ebbets Field.

---

13 f. **All-Scholastic Championship Team of the City of New York:**
Schulauswahlmannschaft der Stadt New York.

24 **incredulously** (adv.): ungläubig.

CHARLEY. Baseball in this weather?

WILLY. Don't talk to him. Come on, come on! *(He is pushing them out.)*

CHARLEY. Wait a minute, didn't you hear the news?

5 WILLY. What?

CHARLEY. Don't you listen to the radio? Ebbets Field just blew up.

WILLY. You go to hell! *(Charley laughs. Pushing them out.)* Come on, come on! We're late.

10 CHARLEY *(as they go)*. Knock a homer, Biff, knock a homer!

WILLY *(the last to leave, turning to Charley)*. I don't think that was funny, Charley. This is the greatest day of his life.

15 CHARLEY. Willy, when are you going to grow up?

WILLY. Yeah, heh? When this game is over, Charley, you'll be laughing out of the other side of your face. They'll be calling him another Red Grange. Twenty-five thousand a year.

20 CHARLEY *(kidding)*. Is that so?

WILLY. Yeah, that's so.

CHARLEY. Well, then, I'm sorry, Willy. But tell me something.

WILLY. What?

25 CHARLEY. Who is Red Grange?

---

7 **to blow up:** explodieren; in die Luft fliegen.

10 **homer** (coll., baseball): *home run:* Schlag, der dem Schläger einen Lauf um sämtliche Male in einem Zug ermöglicht.

17 **you'll be laughing out of the other side of your face** (coll.): dir wird das Lachen schon vergehen.

18 **Grange:** Harold »Red« G. (geb. 1903), legendärer amerikanischer Footballspieler der zwanziger Jahre.

WILLY. Put up your hands. Goddam you, put up your hands!

(Charley, chuckling, shakes his head and walks away, around the left corner of the stage. Willy follows him. The music rises to a mocking frenzy.)

WILLY. Who the hell do you think you are, better than everybody else? You don't know everything, you big, ignorant, stupid ... Put up your hands!

(Light rises, on the right side of the forestage, on a small table in the reception room of Charley's office. Traffic sounds are heard. Bernard, now mature, sits whistling to himself. A pair of tennis rackets and an overnight bag are on the floor beside him.)

WILLY *(offstage)*. What are you walking away for? Don't walk away! If you're going to say something say it to my face! I know you laugh at me behind my back. You'll laugh out of the other side of your goddam face after this game. Touchdown! Touchdown! Eighty thousand people! Touchdown! Right between the goal posts.

(Bernard is a quiet, earnest, but self-assured young man. Willy's voice is coming from right upstage now. Bernard lowers his feet off the table and listens. Jenny, his father's secretary, enters.)

JENNY *(distressed)*. Say, Bernard, will you go out in the hall?

BERNARD. What is that noise? Who is it?

JENNY. Mr. Loman. He just got off the elevator.

---

1 **put up your hands** (coll.): gib's doch auf.
5 **frenzy:** Raserei, Wahnsinn.
12 **racket:** Schläger.
25 **distressed:** besorgt, bekümmert.

BERNARD *(getting up)*. Who's he arguing with?

JENNY. Nobody. There's nobody with him. I can't deal with him any more, and your father gets all upset everytime he comes. I've got a lot of typing to do, and your father's waiting to sign it. Will you see him?

WILLY *(entering)*. Touchdown! Touch – *(He sees Jenny.)* Jenny, Jenny, good to see you. How're ya? Workin'? Or still honest?

JENNY. Fine. How've you been feeling?

WILLY. Not much any more, Jenny. Ha, ha! *(He is surprised to see the rackets.)*

BERNARD. Hello, Uncle Willy.

WILLY *(almost shocked)*. Bernard! Well, look who's here! *(He comes quickly, guiltily, to Bernard and warmly shakes his hand.)*

BERNARD. How are you? Good to see you.

WILLY. What are you doing here?

BERNARD. Oh, just stopped by to see Pop. Get off my feet till my train leaves. I'm going to Washington in a few minutes.

WILLY. Is he in?

BERNARD. Yes, he's in his office with the accountant. Sit down.

WILLY *(sitting down)*. What're you going to do in Washington?

BERNARD. Oh, just a case I've got there, Willy.

WILLY. That so? *(Indicating the rackets.)* You going to play tennis there?

BERNARD. I'm staying with a friend who's got a court.

WILLY. Don't say. His own tennis court. Must be fine people, I bet.

22 **accountant:** Buchhalter.
29 **court:** hier: Tennisplatz.

BERNARD. They are, very nice. Dad tells me Biff's in town.

WILLY *(with a big smile)*. Yeah, Biff's in. Working on a very big deal, Bernard.

5 BERNARD. What's Biff doing?

WILLY. Well, he's been doing very big things in the West. But he decided to establish himself here. Very big. We're having dinner. Did I hear your wife had a boy?

10 BERNARD. That's right. Our second.

WILLY. Two boys! What do you know!

BERNARD. What kind of a deal has Biff got?

WILLY. Well, Bill Oliver – very big sporting-goods man – he wants Biff very badly. Called him in from the

15 West. Long distance, carte blanche, special deliveries. Your friends have their own private tennis court?

BERNARD. You still with the old firm, Willy?

WILLY *(after a pause)*. I'm – I'm overjoyed to see how

20 you made the grade, Bernard, overjoyed. It's an encouraging thing to see a young man really – really – Looks very good for Biff – very – *(He breaks off, then)* Bernard – *(He is so full of emotion, he breaks off again.)*

25 BERNARD. What is it, Willy?

WILLY *(small and alone)*. What – what's the secret?

BERNARD. What secret?

WILLY. How – how did you? Why didn't he ever catch on?

30 BERNARD. I wouldn't know that, Willy.

WILLY *(confidentially, desperately)*. You were his friend,

---

15 **carte blanche** (frz.): (fig.) freie Hand.

his boyhood friend. There's something I don't understand about it. His life ended after that Ebbets Field game. From the age of seventeen nothing good ever happened to him.

BERNARD. He never trained himself for anything.

WILLY. But he did, he did. After high school he took so many correspondence courses. Radio mechanics; television; God knows what, and never made the slightest mark.

BERNARD *(taking off his glasses)*. Willy, do you want to talk candidly?

WILLY *(rising, faces Bernard)*. I regard you as a very brilliant man, Bernard. I value your advice.

BERNARD. Oh, the hell with the advice, Willy. I couldn't advise you. There's just one thing I've always wanted to ask you. When he was supposed to graduate, and the math teacher flunked him –

WILLY. Oh, that son-of-a-bitch ruined his life.

BERNARD. Yeah, but, Willy, all he had to do was go to summer school and make up that subject.

WILLY. That's right, that's right.

BERNARD. Did you tell him not to go to summer school?

WILLY. Me? I begged him to go. I ordered him to go!

BERNARD. Then why wouldn't he go?

WILLY. Why? Why! Bernard, that question has been trailing me like a ghost for the last fifteen years. He flunked the subject, and laid down and died like a hammer hit him!

---

11 **candidly** (adv.): aufrichtig, offen.
20 **to make up:** hier: nachholen.
26 **to trail:** verfolgen.
27 **to lay down:** resignieren, alles fallen lassen.

BERNARD. Take it easy, kid.

WILLY. Let me talk to you – I got nobody to talk to. Bernard, Bernard, was it my fault? Y'see? It keeps going around in my mind, maybe I did something to
5   him. I got nothing to give him.

BERNARD. Don't take it so hard.

WILLY. Why did he lay down? What is the story there? You were his friend!

BERNARD. Willy, I remember, it was June, and our
10   grades came out. And he'd flunked math.

WILLY. That son-of-a-bitch!

BERNARD. No, it wasn't right then. Biff just got very angry, I remember, and he was ready to enroll in summer school.

15   WILLY *(surprised)*. He was?

BERNARD. He wasn't beaten by it at all. But then, Willy, he disappeared from the block for almost a month. And I got the idea that he'd gone up to New England to see you. Did he have a talk with you then?
20   *(Willy stares in silence.)*

BERNARD. Willy?

WILLY *(with a strong edge of resentment in his voice)*. Yeah, he came to Boston. What about it?

BERNARD. Well, just that when he came back – I'll never
25   forget this, it always mystifies me. Because I'd thought so well of Biff, even though he'd always taken advantage of me. I loved him, Willy, y'know? And he came back after that month and took his sneakers – remember those sneakers with "University

---

13 **to enroll:** (sich) eintragen, anmelden für.
25 **to mystify:** Rätsel aufgeben; verwirren.
27 **to take advantage of s.o.:** jdn. ausnutzen, übervorteilen.

of Virginia" printed on them? He was so proud of
those, wore them every day. And he took them down
in the cellar, and burned them up in the furnace. We
had a fist fight. It lasted at least half an hour. Just the
two of us, punching each other down the cellar, and
crying right through it. I've often thought of how
strange it was that I knew he'd given up his life. What
happened in Boston, Willy?
(Willy looks at him as at an intruder.)

BERNARD. I just bring it up because you asked me.

WILLY *(angrily)*. Nothing. What do you mean, "What
happened?" What's that got to do with anything?

BERNARD. Well, don't get sore.

WILLY. What are you trying to do, blame it on me? If a
boy lays down is that my fault?

BERNARD. Now, Willy, don't get –

WILLY. Well, don't – don't talk to me that way! What
does that mean, "What happened?"
*(Charley enters. He is in his vest, and he carries a
bottle of bourbon.)*

CHARLEY. Hey, you're going to miss that train. *(He
waves the bottle.)*

BERNARD. Yeah, I'm going. *(He takes the bottle.)*
Thanks, Pop. *(He picks up his rackets and bag.)*
Good-by, Willy, and don't worry about it. You know,
"If at first you don't succeed ..."

WILLY. Yes, I believe in that.

---

3 **furnace:** Heizungskessel.
9 **intruder:** Störenfried; Eindringling.
13 **sore** (coll.): sauer; eingeschnappt.
14 **to blame s.th. on s.o.:** jdm. die Schuld an etwas zuschieben.
19 **vest:** Unterhemd.
20 **bourbon:** amerikanischer Whiskey.

BERNARD. But sometimes, Willy, it's better for a man just to walk away.

WILLY. Walk away?

BERNARD. That's right.

5 WILLY. But if you can't walk away?

BERNARD *(after a slight pause)*. I guess that's when it's tough. *(Extending his hand.)* Good-by, Willy.

WILLY *(shaking Bernard's hand)*. Good-by, boy.

CHARLEY *(an arm on Bernard's shoulder)*. How do you
10 like this kid? Gonna argue a case in front of the Supreme Court.

BERNARD *(protesting)*. Pop!

WILLY *(genuinely shocked, pained, and happy)*. No! The Supreme Court!

15 BERNARD. I gotta run. 'By, Dad!

CHARLEY. Knock 'em dead, Bernard!

(Bernard goes off.)

WILLY *(as Charley takes out his wallet)*. The Supreme Court! And he didn't even mention it!

20 CHARLEY *(counting out money on the desk)*. He don't have to – he's gonna do it.

WILLY. And you never told him what to do, did you? You never took any interest in him.

CHARLEY. My salvation is that I never took any interest
25 in anything. There's some money – fifty dollars. I got an accountant inside.

WILLY. Charley, look ... *(With difficulty.)* I got my insurance to pay. If you can manage it – I need a hundred and ten dollars.

---

7 **tough:** schwierig, hart.
11 **Supreme Court:** Oberster Bundesgerichtshof.
18 **wallet** (AE): Brieftasche.
24 **salvation:** Rettung.

(Charley doesn't reply for a moment; merely stops moving.)

WILLY. I'd draw it from my bank but Linda would know, and I . . .

CHARLEY. Sit down, Willy.

WILLY *(moving toward the chair)*. I'm keeping an account of everything, remember. I'll pay every penny back. *(He sits.)*

CHARLEY. Now listen to me, Willy.

WILLY. I want you to know I appreciate . . .

CHARLEY *(sitting down on the table)*. Willy, what're you doin'? What the hell is goin' on in your head?

WILLY. Why? I'm simply . . .

CHARLEY. I offered you a job. You can make fifty dollars a week. And I won't send you on the road.

WILLY. I've got a job.

CHARLEY. Without pay? What kind of a job is a job without pay? *(He rises.)* Now, look, kid, enough is enough. I'm no genius but I know when I'm being insulted.

WILLY. Insulted!

CHARLEY. Why don't you want to work for me?

WILLY. What's the matter with you? I've got a job.

CHARLEY. Then what're you walkin' in here every week for?

WILLY *(getting up)*. Well, if you don't want me to walk in here –

CHARLEY. I am offering you a job.

WILLY. I don't want your goddam job!

CHARLEY. When the hell are you going to grow up?

WILLY *(furiously)*. You big ignoramus, if you say that to

---

3 **to draw from:** hier: abheben.

me again I'll rap you one! I don't care how big you
are! *(He's ready to fight.)*
(Pause.)

CHARLEY *(kindly, going to him).* How much do you
need, Willy?

WILLY. Charley, I'm strapped, I'm strapped. I don't
know what to do. I was just fired.

CHARLEY. Howard fired you?

WILLY. That snotnose. Imagine that? I named him. I
named him Howard.

CHARLEY. Willy, when're you gonna realize that them
things don't mean anything? You named him Howard, but you can't sell that. The only thing you got in
this world is what you can sell. And the funny thing is
that you're a salesman, and you don't know that.

WILLY. I've always tried to think otherwise, I guess. I
always felt that if a man was impressive, and well
liked, that nothing –

CHARLEY. Why must everybody like you? Who liked
J. P. Morgan? Was he impressive? In a Turkish bath
he'd look like a butcher. But with his pockets on he
was very well liked. Now listen, Willy, I know you
don't like me, and nobody can say I'm in love with
you, but I'll give you a job because – just for the hell
of it, put it that way. Now what do you say?

WILLY. I – I just can't work for you, Charley.

CHARLEY. What're you, jealous of me?

WILLY. I can't work for you, that's all, don't ask me why.

---

1 **to rap:** schlagen; eins überziehen.
6 **strapped** (coll.): pleite.
9 **snotnose** (coll.): Rotznase; unverschämter Kerl.
20 **Morgan:** John Pierpont M. (1837–1913), amerikanischer Finanzier
und Stahlmagnat.

CHARLEY *(angered, takes out more bills).* You been jealous of me all your life, you damned fool! Here, pay your insurance. *(He puts the money in Willy's hand.)*

WILLY. I'm keeping strict accounts.

CHARLEY. I've got some work to do. Take care of yourself. And pay your insurance.

WILLY *(moving to the right).* Funny, y'know? After all the high-ways, and the trains, and the appointments, and the years, you end up worth more dead than alive.

CHARLEY. Willy, nobody's worth nothin' dead. *(After a slight pause.)* Did you hear what I said?

(Willy stands still, dreaming.)

CHARLEY. Willy!

WILLY. Apologize to Bernard for me when you see him. I didn't mean to argue with him. He's a fine boy. They're all fine boys, and they'll end up big – all of them. Someday they'll all play tennis together. Wish me luck, Charley. He saw Bill Oliver today.

CHARLEY. Good luck.

WILLY *(on the verge of tears).* Charley, you're the only friend I got. Isn't that a remarkable thing? *(He goes out.)*

CHARLEY. Jesus!

(Charley stares after him a moment and follows. All light blacks out. Suddenly raucous music is heard, and a red glow rises behind the screen at right. Stanley, a young waiter, appears, carrying a table, followed by Happy, who is carrying two chairs.)

22 **on the verge of tears:** den Tränen nahe.
27 **raucous:** rauh, heiser.

STANLEY *(putting the table down)*. That's all right, Mr.
Loman, I can handle it myself. *(He turns and takes the
chairs from Happy and places them at the table.)*

HAPPY *(glancing around)*. Oh, this is better.

5 STANLEY. Sure, in the front there you're in the middle
of all kinds a noise. Whenever you got a party,
Mr. Loman, you just tell me and I'll put you back
here. Y'know, there's a lotta people they don't like
it private, because when they go out they like to see

10 a lotta action around them because they're sick and
tired to stay in the house by theirself. But I know
you, you ain't from Hackensack. You know what I
mean?

HAPPY *(sitting down)*. So how's it coming, Stanley?

15 STANLEY. Ah, it's a dog's life. I only wish during the war
they'd a took me in the Army. I coulda been dead by
now.

HAPPY. My brother's back, Stanley.

STANLEY. Oh, he come back, heh? From the Far West.

20 HAPPY. Yeah, big cattle man, my brother, so treat him
right. And my father's coming too.

STANLEY. Oh, your father too!

HAPPY. You got a couple of nice lobsters?

STANLEY. Hundred per cent, big.

25 HAPPY. I want them with the claws.

STANLEY. Don't worry, I don't give you no mice. *(Happy
laughs.)* How about some wine? It'll put a head on
the meal.

---

11 **by theirself:** ungebildet für *by themselves*.
12 **you ain't from Hackensack:** du bist nicht von gestern (*Hackensack:*
Stadt in New Jersey).
23 **lobster:** Hummer.
25 **claw:** Klaue; hier: Schere.

HAPPY. No. You remember, Stanley, that recipe I brought you from overseas? With the champagne in it?

STANLEY. Oh, yeah, sure. I still got it tacked up yet in the kitchen. But that'll have to cost a buck apiece anyways.

HAPPY. That's all right.

STANLEY. What'd you, hit a number or somethin'?

HAPPY. No, it's a little celebration. My brother is – I think he pulled off a big deal today. I think we're going into business together.

STANLEY. Great! That's the best for you. Because a family business, you know what I mean? – that's the best.

HAPPY. That's what I think.

STANLEY. 'Cause what's the difference? Somebody steals? It's in the family. Know what I mean? *(Sotto voce.)* Like this bartender here. The boss is goin' crazy what kinda leak he's got in the cash register. You put it in but it don't come out.

HAPPY *(raising his head)*. Sh!

STANLEY. What?

HAPPY. You notice I wasn't lookin' right or left, was I?

STANLEY. No.

HAPPY. And my eyes are closed.

STANLEY. So what's the –?

HAPPY. Strudel's comin'.

---

4 **to tack up:** anheften.
8 **to hit a number:** in der Lotterie gewinnen.
17 f. **sotto voce** (ital.): mit gedämpfter Stimme.
18 **bartender:** Barmixer.
19 **cash register:** (Registrier-)Kasse.
27 **strudel** (slang): Süße.

STANLEY *(catching on, looks around).* Ah, no, there's no –

(He breaks off as a furred, lavishly dressed girl enters and sits at the next table. Both follow her with their eyes.)

STANLEY. Geez, how'd ya know?

HAPPY. I got radar or something. *(Staring directly at her profile.)* Oooooooo ... Stanley.

STANLEY. I think that's for you, Mr. Loman.

HAPPY. Look at that mouth. Oh, God. And the binoculars.

STANLEY. Geez, you got a life, Mr. Loman.

HAPPY. Wait on her.

STANLEY *(going to the girl's table).* Would you like a menu, ma'am?

GIRL. I'm expecting someone, but I'd like a –

HAPPY. Why don't you bring her – excuse me, miss, do you mind? I sell champagne, and I'd like you to try my brand. Bring her a champagne, Stanley.

GIRL. That's awfully nice of you.

HAPPY. Don't mention it. It's all company money. *(He laughs.)*

GIRL. That's a charming product to be selling, isn't it?

HAPPY. Oh, gets to be like everything else. Selling is selling, y'know.

GIRL. I suppose.

HAPPY. You don't happen to sell, do you?

GIRL. No, I don't sell.

---

3 **furred:** in einem Pelzmantel.
  lavishly (adv.): verschwenderisch.
10f. **binoculars** (pl.): Fernglas; hier (slang): Busen.
19 **brand:** Marke.

HAPPY. Would you object to a compliment from a stranger? You ought to be on a magazine cover.

GIRL *(looking at him a little archly)*. I have been.

(Stanley comes in with a glass of champagne.)

HAPPY. What'd I say before, Stanley? You see? She's a cover girl.

STANLEY. Oh, I could see, I could see.

HAPPY *(to the Girl)*. What magazine?

GIRL. Oh, a lot of them. *(She takes the drink.)* Thank you.

HAPPY. You know what they say in France, don't you? "Champagne is the drink of the complexion" – Hya, Biff!

(Biff has entered and sits with Happy.)

BIFF. Hello, kid. Sorry I'm late.

HAPPY. I just got here. Uh, Miss –?

GIRL. Forsythe.

HAPPY. Miss Forsythe, this is my brother.

BIFF. Is Dad here?

HAPPY. His name is Biff. You might've heard of him. Great football player.

GIRL. Really? What team?

HAPPY. Are you familiar with football?

GIRL. No, I'm afraid I'm not.

HAPPY. Biff is quarterback with the New York Giants.

GIRL. Well, that is nice, isn't it? *(She drinks.)*

HAPPY. Good health.

GIRL. I'm happy to meet you.

---

3 **archly** (adv.): schelmisch; durchtrieben.
12 **complexion:** Gesichtsfarbe; Teint.
25 **quarterback** (Am. football): Ballverteiler und zentraler Spieler.

HAPPY. That's my name. Hap. It's really Harold, but at West Point they called me Happy.

GIRL *(now really impressed)*. Oh, I see. How do you do? *(She turns her profile.)*

5 BIFF. Isn't Dad coming?

HAPPY. You want her?

BIFF. Oh, I could never make that.

HAPPY. I remember the time that idea would never come into your head. Where's the old confidence, Biff?

10 BIFF. I just saw Oliver –

HAPPY. Wait a minute. I've got to see that old confidence again. Do you want her? She's on call.

BIFF. Oh, no. *(He turns to look at the Girl.)*

HAPPY. I'm telling you. Watch this. *(Turning to the Girl.)*

15 Honey? *(She turns to him.)* Are you busy?

GIRL. Well, I am . . . but I could make a phone call.

HAPPY. Do that, will you, honey? And see if you can get a friend. We'll be here for a while. Biff is one of the greatest football players in the country.

20 GIRL *(standing up)*. Well, I'm certainly happy to meet you.

HAPPY. Come back soon.

GIRL. I'll try.

HAPPY. Don't try, honey, try hard.

25 *(The Girl exits. Stanley follows, shaking his head in bewildered admiration.)*

HAPPY. Isn't that a shame now? A beautiful girl like that? That's why I can't get married. There's not a good woman in a thousand. New York is loaded with

30 them, kid!

BIFF. Hap, look –

2 **West Point:** Militärakademie im Staate New York.

HAPPY. I told you she was on call!

BIFF *(strangely unnerved)*. Cut it out, will ya? I want to say something to you.

HAPPY. Did you see Oliver?

5 BIFF. I saw him all right. Now look, I want to tell Dad a couple of things and I want you to help me.

HAPPY. What? Is he going to back you?

BIFF. Are you crazy? You're out of your goddam head, you know that?

10 HAPPY. Why? What happened?

BIFF *(breathlessly)*. I did a terrible today, Hap. It's been the strangest day I ever went through. I'm all numb, I swear.

HAPPY. You mean he wouldn't see you?

15 BIFF. Well, I waited six hours for him, see? All day. Kept sending my name in. Even tried to date his secretary so she'd get me to him, but no soap.

HAPPY. Because you're not showin' the old confidence, Biff. He remembered you, didn't he?

20 BIFF *(stopping Happy with a gesture)*. Finally, about five o'clock, he comes out. Didn't remember who I was or anything. I felt like such an idiot, Hap.

HAPPY. Did you tell him my Florida idea?

BIFF. He walked away. I saw him for one minute. I got

25 so mad I could've torn the walls down! How the hell did I ever get the idea I was a salesman there? I even believed myself that I'd been a salesman for him! And then he gave me one look and – I realized what a ridiculous lie my whole life has been! We've been

---

2 **cut it out:** hör auf!, laß es!

8 **to be out of one's head:** verrückt sein.

17 **no soap** (slang): da lief nichts.

talking in a dream for fifteen years. I was a shipping
clerk.

HAPPY. What'd you do?

BIFF *(with great tension and wonder)*. Well, he left, see.
5   And the secretary went out. I was all alone in the
waiting-room. I don't know what came over me,
Hap. The next thing I know I'm in his office –
paneled walls, everything. I can't explain it. I – Hap,
I took his fountain pen.

10 HAPPY. Geez, did he catch you?

BIFF. I ran out. I ran down all eleven flights. I ran and
ran and ran.

HAPPY. That was an awful dumb – what'd you do that
for?

15 BIFF *(agonized)*. I don't know, I just – wanted to take
something, I don't know. You gotta help me, Hap,
I'm gonna tell Pop.

HAPPY. You crazy? What for?

BIFF. Hap, he's got to understand that I'm not the man
20   somebody lends that kind of money to. He thinks I've
been spiting him all these years and it's eating him up.

HAPPY. That's just it. You tell him something nice.

BIFF. I can't.

HAPPY. Say you got a lunch date with Oliver tomorrow.

25 BIFF. So what do I do tomorrow?

HAPPY. You leave the house tomorrow and come back at
night and say Oliver is thinking it over. And he

---

4 **tension:** Anspannung.
8 **paneled:** getäfelt.
11 **flight** (*of stairs*): Treppe.
13 **dumb** (coll.): dumm, blöd.
15 **agonized:** verzweifelt; gequält.
21 **to spite s.o.:** jdn. ärgern; trotzen.

thinks it over for a couple of weeks, and gradually it
fades away and nobody's the worse.

BIFF. But it'll go on forever!

HAPPY. Dad is never so happy as when he's looking
forward to something!

(Willy enters.)

HAPPY. Hello, scout!

WILLY. Gee, I haven't been here in years!

*(Stanley has followed Willy in and sets a chair for him.
Stanley starts off but Happy stops him.)*

HAPPY. Stanley!

(Stanley stands by, waiting for an order.)

BIFF *(going to Willy with guilt, as to an invalid)*. Sit
down, Pop. You want a drink?

WILLY. Sure, I don't mind.

BIFF. Let's get a load on.

WILLY. You look worried.

BIFF. N-no. *(To Stanley.)* Scotch all around. Make it
doubles.

STANLEY. Doubles, right. *(He goes.)*

WILLY. You had a couple already, didn't you?

BIFF. Just a couple, yeah.

WILLY. Well, what happened, boy? *(Nodding affirmatively, with a smile.)* Everything go all right?

BIFF *(takes a breath, then reaches out and grasps Willy's
hand)*. Pal ... *(He is smiling bravely, and Willy is
smiling too.)* I had an experience today.

HAPPY. Terrific, Pop.

WILLY. That so? What happened?

---

2 **nobody's the worse:** keinem hat's geschadet.
13 **guilt:** Schuldbewußtsein.
23 f. **affirmatively** (adv.): bejahend, bekräftigend.

BIFF *(high, slightly alcoholic, above the earth).* I'm going
to tell you everything from first to last. It's been a
strange day. *(Silence. He looks around, composes
himself as best he can, but his breath keeps breaking
the rhythm of his voice.)* I had to wait quite a while for
him, and –

WILLY. Oliver?

BIFF. Yeah, Oliver. All day, as a matter of cold fact.
And a lot of – instances – facts, Pop, facts about my
life came back to me. Who was it, Pop? Who ever
said I was a salesman with Oliver?

WILLY. Well, you were.

BIFF. No, Dad, I was a shipping clerk.

WILLY. But you were practically –

BIFF *(with determination).* Dad, I don't know who said it
first, but I was never a salesman for Bill Oliver.

WILLY. What're you talking about?

BIFF. Let's hold on to the facts tonight, Pop. We're not
going to get anywhere bullin' around. I was a shipping clerk.

WILLY *(angrily).* All right, now listen to me –

BIFF. Why don't you let me finish?

WILLY. I'm not interested in stories about the past or any
crap of that kind because the woods are burning,
boys, you understand? There's a big blaze going on
all around. I was fired today.

BIFF *(shocked).* How could you be?

WILLY. I was fired, and I'm looking for a little good news

---

3 f. **to compose o.s.:** sich fassen, sich beruhigen.
19 **to bull around** (slang): herumreden; Unfug quasseln.
24 **crap** (vulg.): Scheiße.
25 **there's a big blaze:** (fig.) es brennt lichterloh.

to tell your mother, because the woman has waited
and the woman has suffered. The gist of it is that I
haven't got a story left in my head, Biff. So don't give
me a lecture about facts and aspects. I am not interested. Now what've you got to say to me?
*(Stanley enters with three drinks. They wait until he
leaves.)*

WILLY. Did you see Oliver?

BIFF. Jesus, Dad!

WILLY. You mean you didn't go up there?

HAPPY. Sure he went up there.

BIFF. I did. I – saw him. How could they fire you?

WILLY *(on the edge of his chair)*. What kind of a welcome
did he give you?

BIFF. He won't even let you work on commission?

WILLY. I'm out! *(Driving.)* So tell me, he gave you a
warm welcome?

HAPPY. Sure, Pop, sure!

BIFF *(driven)*. Well, it was kind of –

WILLY. I was wondering if he'd remember you. *(To
Happy.)* Imagine, man doesn't see him for ten,
twelve years and gives him that kind of a welcome!

HAPPY. Damn right!

BIFF *(trying to return to the offensive)*. Pop, look –

WILLY. You know why he remembered you, don't you?
Because you impressed him in those days.

BIFF. Let's talk quietly and get this down to the facts,
huh?

WILLY *(as though Biff had been interrupting)*. Well, what

---

2 **gist:** Hauptpunkt, Kern.
16 **driving:** drängend.

happened? It's great news, Biff. Did he take you into
his office or'd you talk in the waiting-room?

BIFF. Well, he came in, see, and –

WILLY *(with a big smile)*. What'd he say? Betcha he
5   threw his arm around you.

BIFF. Well, he kinda –

WILLY. He's a fine man. *(To Happy.)* Very hard man to
see, y'know.

HAPPY *(agreeing)*. Oh, I know.

10   WILLY *(to Biff)*. Is that where you had the drinks?

BIFF. Yeah, he gave me a couple of – no, no!

HAPPY *(cutting in)*. He told him my Florida idea.

WILLY. Don't interrupt. *(To Biff.)* How'd he react to the
Florida idea?

15   BIFF. Dad, will you give me a minute to explain?

WILLY. I've been waiting for you to explain since I sat
down here! What happened? He took you into his
office and what?

BIFF. Well – I talked. And – and he listened, see.

20   WILLY. Famous for the way he listens, y'know. What was
his answer?

BIFF. His answer was – *(He breaks off, suddenly angry.)*
Dad, you're not letting me tell you what I want to tell
you!

25   WILLY *(accusing, angered)*. You didn't see him, did you?

BIFF. I did see him!

WILLY. What'd you insult him or something? You
insulted him, didn't you?

BIFF. Listen, will you let me out of it, will you just let me
30   out of it!

---

4 **betcha** (slang): *I bet you:* ich wette.
12 **to cut in:** unterbrechen.
29 **will you let me out of it:** laß mich doch damit zufrieden.

HAPPY. What the hell!

WILLY. Tell me what happened!

BIFF *(to Happy)*. I can't talk to him!

(A single trumpet note jars the ear. The light of green leaves stains the house, which holds the air of night and a dream. Young Bernard enters and knocks on the door of the house.)

YOUNG BERNARD *(frantically)*. Mrs. Loman, Mrs. Loman!

HAPPY. Tell him what happened!

BIFF *(to Happy)*. Shut up and leave me alone!

WILLY. No, no! You had to go and flunk math!

BIFF. What math? What're you talking about?

YOUNG BERNARD. Mrs. Loman, Mrs. Loman!

(Linda appears in the house, as of old.)

WILLY *(wildly)*. Math, math, math!

BIFF. Take it easy, Pop!

YOUNG BERNARD. Mrs. Loman!

WILLY *(furiously)*. If you hadn't flunked you'd've been set by now!

BIFF. Now, look, I'm gonna tell you what happened, and you're going to listen to me.

YOUNG BERNARD. Mrs. Loman!

BIFF. I waited six hours –

HAPPY. What the hell are you saying?

BIFF. I kept sending in my name but he wouldn't see me. So finally he . . . *(He continues unheard as light fades low on the restaurant.)*

YOUNG BERNARD. Biff flunked math!

LINDA. No!

---

4 **to jar:** unangenehm berühren; verletzen.

5 **to stain:** hier: in Farbe tauchen.

8 **frantically** (adv.), wild, ungestüm.

YOUNG BERNARD. Birnbaum flunked him! They won't graduate him!

LINDA. But they have to. He's gotta go to the university. Where is he? Biff! Biff!

5 YOUNG BERNARD. No, he left. He went to Grand Central.

LINDA. Grand – You mean he went to Boston!

YOUNG BERNARD. Is Uncle Willy in Boston?

LINDA. Oh, maybe Willy can talk to the teacher. Oh, the
10   poor, poor boy!

(Light on house area snaps out.)

BIFF *(at the table, now audible, holding up a gold fountain pen)*. ... so I'm washed up with Oliver, you understand? Are you listening to me?

15 WILLY *(at a loss)*. Yeah, sure. If you hadn't flunked –

BIFF. Flunked what? What're you talking about?

WILLY. Don't blame everything on me! I didn't flunk math – you did! What pen?

HAPPY. That was awful dumb, Biff, a pen like that is
20   worth –

WILLY *(seeing the pen for the first time)*. You took Oliver's pen?

BIFF *(weakening)*. Dad, I just explained it to you.

WILLY. You stole Bill Oliver's fountain pen!

25 BIFF. I didn't exactly steal it! That's just what I've been explaining to you!

HAPPY. He had it in his hand and just then Oliver walked in, so he got nervous and stuck it in his pocket!

WILLY. My God, Biff!

30 BIFF. I never intended to do it, Dad!

---

12 **audible:** hörbar.
13 **to be washed up with s.o.** (AE): mit jdm. fertig sein.

OPERATOR'S VOICE. Standish Arms, good evening!

WILLY *(shouting)*. I'm not in my room!

BIFF *(frightened)*. Dad, what's the matter? *(He and Happy stand up.)*

5 OPERATOR. Ringing Mr. Loman for you!

WILLY. I'm not there, stop it!

BIFF *(horrified, gets down on one knee before Willy)*. Dad, I'll make good, I'll make good. *(Willy tries to get to his feet. Biff holds him down.)* Sit down now.

10 WILLY. No, you're no good, you're no good for anything.

BIFF. I am, Dad, I'll find something else, you understand? Now don't worry about anything. *(He holds up Willy's face.)* Talk to me, Dad.

15 OPERATOR. Mr. Loman does not answer. Shall I page him?

WILLY *(attempting to stand, as though to rush and silence the Operator)*. No, no, no!

HAPPY. He'll strike something, Pop.

20 WILLY. No, no . . .

BIFF *(desperately, standing over Willy)*. Pop, listen! Listen to me! I'm telling you something good. Oliver talked to his partner about the Florida idea. You listening? He – he talked to his partner, and he came

25 to me . . . I'm going to be all right, you hear? Dad, listen to me, he said it was just a question of the amount!

WILLY. Then you . . . got it?

HAPPY. He's gonna be terrific, Pop!

---

1 **operator:** Telefonist(in).
  Standish Arms: Name eines Hotels.
15 **to page s.o.:** jdn. ausrufen lassen.

WILLY *(trying to stand)*. Then you got it, haven't you?
You got it! You got it!

BIFF *(agonized, holds Willy down)*. No, no. Look, Pop.
I'm supposed to have lunch with them tomorrow. I'm
5   just telling you this so you'll know that I can still
make an impression, Pop. And I'll make good somewhere, but I can't go tomorrow, see?

WILLY. Why not? You simply –

BIFF. But the pen, Pop!

10 WILLY. You give it to him and tell him it was an
oversight!

HAPPY. Sure, have lunch tomorrow!

BIFF. I can't say that –

WILLY. You were doing a crossword puzzle and acciden-
15   tally used his pen!

BIFF. Listen, kid, I took those balls years ago, now I
walk in with his fountain pen? That clinches it, don't
you see? I can't face him like that! I'll try elsewhere.

PAGE'S VOICE. Paging Mr. Loman!

20 WILLY. Don't you want to be anything?

BIFF. Pop, how can I go back?

WILLY. You don't want to be anything, is that what's behind it?

BIFF *(now angry at Willy for not crediting his sympathy)*.
25   Don't take it that way! You think it was easy walking
into that office after what I'd done to him? A team of
horses couldn't have dragged me back to Bill Oliver!

WILLY. Then why'd you go?

---

11 **oversight:** Versehen.
14 **crossword puzzle:** Kreuzworträtsel.
17 **to clinch:** entscheiden; endgültig regeln.
24 **to credit s.o.'s sympathy:** jds. Sympathie, Zuneigung akzeptieren.

BIFF. Why did I go? Why did I go! Look at you! Look at what's become of you!
   (Off left, The Woman laughs.)

WILLY. Biff, you're going to go to that lunch tomorrow, or –

BIFF. I can't go. I've got no appointment!

HAPPY. Biff, for . . . !

WILLY. Are you spiting me?

BIFF. Don't take it that way! Goddammit!

WILLY *(strikes Biff and falters away from the table)*. You rotten little louse! Are you spiting me?

THE WOMAN. Someone's at the door, Willy!

BIFF. I'm no good, can't you see what I am?

HAPPY *(separating them)*. Hey, you're in a restaurant! Now cut it out, both of you? *(The girls enter.)* Hello, girls, sit down.
   (The Woman laughs, off left.)

MISS FORSYTHE. I guess we might as well. This is Letta.

THE WOMAN. Willy, are you going to wake up?

BIFF *(ignoring Willy)*. How're ya, miss, sit down. What do you drink?

MISS FORSYTHE. Letta might not be able to stay long.

LETTA. I gotta get up very early tomorrow. I got jury duty. I'm so excited! Were you fellows ever on a jury?

BIFF. No, but I been in front of them! *(The girls laugh.)* This is my father.

LETTA. Isn't he cute? Sit down with us, Pop.

---

10 **to falter:** straucheln.
11 **louse:** Laus.
23 f. **I got jury duty:** Ich bin als Geschworene geladen.
28 **cute** (AE): nett, niedlich.

HAPPY. Sit him down, Biff!

BIFF *(going to him)*. Come on, slugger, drink us under
the table. To hell with it! Come on, sit down, pal.
(On Biff's last insistence, Willy is about to sit.)

5 THE WOMAN *(now urgently)*. Willy, are you going to
answer the door!
*(The Woman's call pulls Willy back. He starts right,
befuddled.)*

BIFF. Hey, where are you going?

10 WILLY. Open the door.

BIFF. The door?

WILLY. The washroom ... the door ... where's the
door?

BIFF *(leading Willy to the left)*. Just go straight down.

15 *(Willy moves left.)*

THE WOMAN. Willy, Willy, are you going to get up, get
up, get up, get up?
(Willy exits left.)

LETTA. I think it's sweet you bring your daddy along.

20 MISS FORSYTHE. Oh, he isn't really your father!

BIFF *(at left, turning to her resentfully)*. Miss Forsythe,
you've just seen a prince walk by. A fine, troubled
prince. A hardworking, unappreciated prince. A pal,
you understand? A good companion. Always for his

25 boys.

LETTA. That's so sweet.

HAPPY. Well, girls, what's the program? We're wasting

---

2 **slugger** (AE, coll.): jd., der hart zuschlägt; (im Baseball) ein harter
Schläger.

5 **urgently** (adv.): dringlich.

8 **befuddled:** verwirrt; betrunken.

21 **resentfully** (adv.): gereizt; verächtlich.

time. Come on, Biff. Gather round. Where would
you like to go?

BIFF. Why don't you do something for him?

HAPPY. Me!

5 BIFF. Don't you give a damn for him, Hap?

HAPPY. What're you talking about? I'm the one who –

BIFF. I sense it, you don't give a good goddam about
him. *(He takes the rolled-up hose from his pocket and
puts it on the table in front of Happy.)* Look what I

10 found in the cellar, for Christ's sake. How can you
bear to let it go on?

HAPPY. Me? Who goes away? Who runs off and –

BIFF. Yeah, but he doesn't mean anything to you. You
could help him – I can't! Don't you understand what

15 I'm talking about? He's going to kill himself, don't
you know that?

HAPPY. Don't I know it! Me!

BIFF. Hap, help him! Jesus ... help him ... Help me,
help me, I can't bear to look at his face! *(Ready to*

20 *weep, he hurries out, up right.)*

HAPPY *(starting after him)*. Where are you going?

MISS FORSYTHE. What's he so mad about?

HAPPY. Come on, girls, we'll catch up with him.

MISS FORSYTHE *(as Happy pushes her out)*. Say, I don't

25 like that temper of his!

HAPPY. He's just a little overstrung, he'll be all right!

WILLY *(off left, as The Woman laughs)*. Don't answer!
Don't answer!

LETTA. Don't you want to tell your father –

---

5 **don't give a damn** (vulg.): einen Dreck auf etwas geben.
8 **hose:** Schlauch.
26 **overstrung:** überreizt; überanstrengt.

HAPPY. No, that's not my father. He's just a guy. Come
on, we'll catch Biff, and, honey, we're going to paint
this town! Stanley, where's the check! Hey, Stanley!
(They exit. Stanley looks toward left.)
5 STANLEY *(calling to Happy indignantly)*. Mr. Loman!
Mr. Loman!
*(Stanley picks up a chair and follows them off. Knock-
ing is heard off left. The Woman enters, laughing.
Willy follows her. She is in a black slip; he is buttoning
10 his shirt. Raw, sensuous music accompanies their
speech.)*
WILLY. Will you stop laughing? Will you stop?
THE WOMAN. Aren't you going to answer the door? He'll
wake the whole hotel.
15 WILLY. I'm not expecting anybody.
THE WOMAN. Whyn't you have another drink, honey,
and stop being so damn self-centered?
WILLY. I'm so lonely.
THE WOMAN. You know you ruined me, Willy? From
20 now on, whenever you come to the office, I'll see that
you go right through to the buyers. No waiting at my
desk any more, Willy. You ruined me.
WILLY. That's nice of you to say that.
THE WOMAN. Gee, you are self-centered! Why so sad?
25 You are the saddest, self-centeredest soul I ever did
see-saw. *(She laughs. He kisses her.)* Come on inside,
drummer boy. It's silly to be dressing in the middle of

---

2 f. **to paint the town** (slang): auf die Pauke hauen; auf Sauftour gehen.
10 **sensuous:** sinnlich.
16 **whyn't you** (slang): *why don't you.*
17 **self-centered:** egozentrisch, ichbezogen.
25 f. **I ever did see-saw:** Wortspiel mit Präs./Imperf. von *to see* ›kennen‹
und *see-saw* ›Wippe; Auf-und-ab-Bewegung‹.

the night. *(As knocking is heard.)* Aren't you going to
answer the door?

WILLY. They're knocking on the wrong door.

THE WOMAN. But I felt the knocking. And he heard us
talking in here. Maybe the hotel's on fire!

WILLY *(his terror rising)*. It's a mistake.

THE WOMAN. Then tell him to go away!

WILLY. There's nobody there.

THE WOMAN. It's getting on my nerves, Willy. There's
somebody standing out there and it's getting on my
nerves!

WILLY *(pushing her away from him)*. All right, stay in
the bathroom here, and don't come out. I think
there's a law in Massachusetts about it, so don't come
out. It may be that new room clerk. He looked very
mean. So don't come out. It's a mistake, there's no
fire.

*(The knocking is heard again. He takes a few steps
away from her, and she vanishes into the wing. The
light follows him, and now he is facing Young Biff,
who carries a suitcase. Biff steps toward him. The
music is gone.)*

BIFF. Why didn't you answer?

WILLY. Biff! What are you doing in Boston?

BIFF. Why didn't you answer? I've been knocking for
five minutes, I called you on the phone –

WILLY. I just heard you. I was in the bathroom and had
the door shut. Did anything happen home?

BIFF. Dad – I let you down.

WILLY. What do you mean?

BIFF. Dad . . .

---

29 **to let s.o. down:** jdn. im Stich lassen, enttäuschen.

WILLY. Biffo, what's this about? *(Putting his arm around Biff.)* Come on, let's go downstairs and get you a malted.

BIFF. Dad, I flunked math.

5 WILLY. Not for the term?

BIFF. The term. I haven't got enough credits to graduate.

WILLY. You mean to say Bernard wouldn't give you the answers?

BIFF. He did, he tried, but I only got a sixty-one.

10 WILLY. And they wouldn't give you four points?

BIFF. Birnbaum refused absolutely. I begged him, Pop, but he won't give me those points. You gotta talk to him before they close the school. Because if he saw the kind of man you are, and you just talked to him in
15 your way, I'm sure he'd come through for me. The class came right before practice, see, and I didn't go enough. Would you talk to him? He'd like you, Pop. You know the way you could talk.

WILLY. You're on. We'll drive right back.

20 BIFF. Oh, Dad, good work! I'm sure he'll change it for you!

WILLY. Go downstairs and tell the clerk I'm checkin' out. Go right down.

BIFF. Yes, sir! See, the reason he hates me, Pop – one
25 day he was late for class so I got up at the blackboard and imitated him. I crossed my eyes and talked with a lithp.

---

3 **malted:** Abk. für *malted milk* ›Milchgetränk mit Malzgeschmack‹.
6 **credits:** Punkte für das Abschlußexamen.
19 **you're on:** einverstanden, wird gemacht.
22 f. **to check out:** (aus einem Hotel) abreisen.
26 **to cross one's eyes:** schielen.
27 **lithp:** *lisp:* Lispeln.

WILLY *(laughing)*. You did? The kids like it?

BIFF. They nearly died laughing!

WILLY. Yeah? What'd you do?

BIFF. The thquare root of thixthy twee is ... *(Willy*
5 *bursts out laughing; Biff joins him.)* And in the middle of it he walked in!

(Willy laughs and The Woman joins in offstage.)

WILLY *(without hesitation)*. Hurry downstairs and –

BIFF. Somebody in there?

10 WILLY. No, that was next door.

(The Woman laughs offstage.)

BIFF. Somebody got in your bathroom!

WILLY. No, it's the next room, there's a party –

THE WOMAN *(enters, laughing. She lisps this.)* Can I come
15 in? There's something in the bathtub, Willy, and it's
moving!

*(Willy looks at Biff, who is staring open-mouthed and
horrified at The Woman.)*

WILLY. Ah – you better go back to your room. They
20 must be finished painting by now. They're painting
her room so I let her take a shower here. Go back, go
back ... *(He pushes her.)*

THE WOMAN *(resisting)*. But I've got to get dressed,
Willy, I can't –

25 WILLY. Get out of here! Go back, go back ... *(Suddenly
striving for the ordinary)*. This is Miss Francis, Biff,
she's a buyer. They're painting her room. Go back,
Miss Francis, go back ...

THE WOMAN. But my clothes, I can't go out naked in the
30 hall!

---

4 **thquare:** *square.*
15 **bathtub:** Badewanne.
26 **striving for the ordinary:** sich um Beiläufigkeit bemühend.

WILLY *(pushing her offstage).* Get outa here! Go back,
go back!
*(Biff slowly sits down on his suitcase as the argument
continues offstage.)*
5 THE WOMAN. Where's my stockings? You promised me
stockings, Willy!
WILLY. I have no stockings here!
THE WOMAN. You had two boxes of size nine sheers for
me, and I want them!
10 WILLY. Here, for God's sake, will you get outa here!
THE WOMAN *(enters holding a box of stockings).* I just
hope there's nobody in the hall. That's all I hope. *(To
Biff.)* Are you football or baseball?
BIFF. Football.
15 THE WOMAN *(angry, humiliated).* That's me too. G'night.
(She snatches her clothes from Willy, and walks out.)
WILLY *(after a pause).* Well, better get going. I want to
get to the school first thing in the morning. Get my
suits out of the closet. I'll get my valise. *(Biff doesn't
20 move.)* What's the matter? *(Biff remains motionless,
tears falling.)* She's a buyer. Buys for J. H. Simmons.
She lives down the hall – they're painting. You don't
imagine – *(He breaks off. After a pause.)* Now listen,
pal, she's just a buyer. She sees merchandise in her
25 room and they have to keep it looking just so ...
(Pause. Assuming command.) All right, get my suits.
(Biff doesn't move.) Now stop crying and do as I say.
I gave you an order. Biff, I gave you an order! Is that

---

8 **sheers:** Nylonstrümpfe.
15 **humiliated:** gedemütigt.
19 **closet:** Schrank.
26 **assuming command:** das Kommando übernehmend.

what you do when I give you an order? How dare you cry! *(Putting his arm around Biff.)* Now look, Biff, when you grow up you'll understand about these things. You mustn't – you mustn't overemphasize a thing like this. I'll see Birnbaum first thing in the morning.

BIFF. Never mind.

WILLY *(getting down beside Biff)*. Never mind! He's going to give you those points. I'll see to it.

BIFF. He wouldn't listen to you.

WILLY. He certainly will listen to me. You need those points for the U. of Virginia.

BIFF. I'm not going there.

WILLY. Heh? If I can't get him to change that mark you'll make it up in summer school. You've got all summer to –

BIFF *(his weeping breaking from him)*. Dad . . .

WILLY *(infected by it)*. Oh, my boy . . .

BIFF. Dad . . .

WILLY. She's nothing to me, Biff. I was lonely, I was terribly lonely.

BIFF. You – you gave her Mama's stockings! *(His tears break through and he rises to go.)*

WILLY *(grabbing for Biff)*. I gave you an order!

BIFF. Don't touch me, you – liar!

WILLY. Apologize for that!

BIFF. You fake! You phony little fake! You fake! *(Overcome, he turns quickly and weeping fully goes out with his suitcase. Willy is left on the floor on his knees.)*

---

4 **to overemphasize:** überbetonen.
27 **phony** (coll.): falsch, unecht; heuchlerisch.

WILLY. I gave you an order! Biff, come back here or I'll
    beat you! Come back here! I'll whip you!
    *(Stanley comes quickly in from the right and stands in
    front of Willy.)*
5 WILLY *(shouts at Stanley)*. I gave you an order . . .
STANLEY. Hey, let's pick it up, pick it up, Mr. Loman.
    (He helps Willy to his feet.) Your boys left with the
    chippies. They said they'll see you home.
    (A second waiter watches some distance away.)
10 WILLY. But we were supposed to have dinner together.
    (Music is heard, Willy's theme.)
STANLEY. Can you make it?
WILLY. I'll – sure, I can make it. *(Suddenly concerned
    about his clothes.)* Do I – I look all right?
15 STANLEY. Sure, you look all right. *(He flicks a speck off
    Willy's lapel.)*
WILLY. Here – here's a dollar.
STANLEY. Oh, your son paid me. It's all right.
WILLY *(putting it in Stanley's hand)*. No, take it. You're
20   a good boy.
STANLEY. Oh, no, you don't have to . . .
WILLY. Here – here's some more, I don't need it any
    more. *(After a slight pause)*. Tell me – is there a seed
    store in the neighborhood?
25 STANLEY. Seeds? You mean like to plant?
    *(As Willy turns, Stanley slips the money back into his
    jacket pocket.)*
WILLY. Yes. Carrots, peas . . .

---

6 **let's pick it up:** hier: wir wollen uns mal zusammenreißen.
8 **chippy:** Flittchen, Prostituierte.
15 **to flick off:** wegschnippen; abklopfen.
   speck: Fleck, Fluse.
16 **lapel:** Revers; Kragenaufschlag.

STANLEY. Well, there's hardware stores on Sixth Avenue, but it may be too late now.

WILLY *(anxiously).* Oh, I'd better hurry. I've got to get some seeds. *(He starts off to the right.)* I've got to get some seeds, right away. Nothing's planted. I don't have a thing in the ground.

(Willy hurries out as the light goes down. Stanley moves over to the right after him, watches him off. The other waiter has been staring at Willy.)

STANLEY *(to the waiter).* Well, whatta you looking at?

(The waiter picks up the chairs and moves off right. Stanley takes the table and follows him. The light fades on this area. There is a long pause, the sound of the flute coming over. The light gradually rises on the kitchen, which is empty. Happy appears at the door of the house, followed by Biff. Happy is carrying a large bunch of long-stemmed roses. He enters the kitchen, looks around for Linda. Not seeing her, he turns to Biff, who is just outside the house door, and makes a gesture with his hands, indicating "Not here, I guess." He looks into the living-room and freezes. Inside, Linda, unseen, is seated, Willy's coat on her lap. She rises ominously and quietly and moves toward Happy, who backs up into the kitchen, afraid.)

HAPPY. Hey, what're you doing up? *(Linda says nothing but moves toward him implacably.)* Where's Pop? *(He keeps backing to the right, and now Linda is in full view in the doorway to the living-room.)* Is he sleeping?

---

1 **hardware store:** Eisenwarenhandlung.
17 **long-stemmed:** langstielig.
23 **ominously** (adv.): unheilvoll, unheilverheißend.
26 **implacably** (adv.): unerbittlich, unversöhnlich.

LINDA. Where were you?

HAPPY *(trying to laugh it off).* We met two girls, Mom,
very fine types. Here, we brought you some flowers.
(Offering them to her.) Put them in your room, Ma.
5   *(She knocks them to the floor at Biff's feet. He has
now come inside and closed the door behind him. She
stares at Biff, silent.)*

HAPPY. Now what'd you do that for? Mom, I want you to
have some flowers –

10   LINDA *(cutting Happy off, violently to Biff.)* Don't you
care whether he lives or dies?

HAPPY *(going to the stairs).* Come upstairs, Biff.

BIFF *(with a flare of disgust, to Happy).* Go away from
me! *(To Linda.)* What do you mean, lives or dies?
15   Nobody's dying around here, pal.

LINDA. Get out of my sight! Get out of here!

BIFF. I wanna see the boss.

LINDA. You're not going near him!

BIFF. Where is he? *(He moves into the living-room and
20   Linda follows.)*

LINDA *(shouting after Biff).* You invite him for dinner.
He looks forward to it all day – *(Biff appears in his
parents' bedroom, looks around, and exits)* – and then
you desert him there. There's no stranger you'd do
25   that to!

HAPPY. Why? He had a swell time with us. Listen, when
I – *(Linda comes back into the kitchen)* – desert him I
hope I don't outlive the day!

LINDA. Get out of here!

---

13 **with a flare of disgust:** mit aufflammendem Ekel.
26 **swell** (slang): prima, dufte, bombig.
28 **to outlive:** überleben.

HAPPY. Now look, Mom . . .

LINDA. Did you have to go to women tonight? You and
your lousy rotten whores!
(Biff re-enters the kitchen.)

5 HAPPY. Mom, all we did was follow Biff around trying to
cheer him up! *(To Biff.)* Boy, what a night you gave
me!

LINDA. Get out of here, both of you, and don't come
back! I don't want you tormenting him any more. Go

10 on now, get your things together! *(To Biff.)* You can't
sleep in his apartment. *(She starts to pick up the
flowers and stops herself.)* Pick up this stuff, I'm not
your maid any more. Pick it up, you bum, you!
(Happy turns his back to her in refusal. Biff slowly

15 *moves over and gets down on his knees, picking up the
flowers.)*

LINDA. You're a pair of animals! Not one, not another
living soul would have had the cruelty to walk out on
that man in a restaurant!

20 BIFF *(not looking at her).* Is that what he said?

LINDA. He didn't have to say anything. He was so
humiliated he nearly limped when he came in.

HAPPY. But, Mom, he had a great time with us –

BIFF *(cutting him off violently).* Shut up!

25 *(Without another word, Happy goes upstairs.)*

LINDA. You! You didn't even go in to see if he was all
right!

BIFF *(still on the floor in front of Linda, the flowers in
his hand; with self-loathing).* No. Didn't. Didn't do a

---

3 **whore:** Hure.

18 **to walk out on s.o.** (coll.): jdn. im Stich lassen.

22 **to limp:** hinken; hier: niedergeschlagen einherschleichen.

29 **self-loathing:** Selbstverachtung.

damned thing. How do you like that, heh? Left him
babbling in a toilet.

LINDA. You louse. You . . .

BIFF. Now you hit it on the nose! *(He gets up, throws the
flowers in the wastebasket.)* The scum of the earth,
and you're looking at him!

LINDA. Get out of here!

BIFF. I gotta talk to the boss, Mom. Where is he?

LINDA. You're not going near him. Get out of this house!

BIFF *(with absolute assurance, determination).* No.
We're gonna have an abrupt conversation, him and
me.

LINDA. You're not talking to him!

*(Hammering is heard from outside the house, off
right. Biff turns toward the noise.)*

LINDA *(suddenly pleading).* Will you please leave him
alone?

BIFF. What's he doing out there?

LINDA. He's planting the garden!

BIFF *(quietly).* Now? Oh, my God!

*(Biff moves outside, Linda following. The light dies
down on them and comes up on the center of the apron
as Willy walks into it. He is carrying a flashlight, a
hoe, and a handful of seed packets. He raps the top of
the hoe sharply to fix it firmly, and then moves to the
left, measuring off the distance with his foot. He holds
the flashlight to look at the seed packets, reading off
the instructions. He is in the blue of night.)*

---

2 **to babble:** lallen, stammeln.
4 **you hit it on the nose:** du triffst den Nagel auf den Kopf.
5 **scum of the earth:** Abschaum der Menschheit.
23 **flashlight** (AE): Taschenlampe.
24 **hoe:** Hacke.

WILLY. Carrots ... quarter-inch apart. Rows ... one-
foot rows. *(He measures it off.)* One foot. *(He puts
down a package and measures off.)* Beets. *(He puts
down another package and measures again.)* Lettuce.
(He reads the package, puts it down.) One foot – *(He
breaks off as Ben appears at the right and moves
slowly down to him.)* What a proposition, ts, ts.
Terrific, terrific. 'Cause she's suffered, Ben, the
woman has suffered. You understand me? A man
can't go out the way he came in, Ben, a man has got
to add up to something. You can't, you can't – *(Ben
moves toward him as though to interrupt.)* You gotta
consider, now. Don't answer so quick. Remember,
it's a guaranteed twenty-thousand-dollar proposition. Now look, Ben, I want you to go through the
ins and outs of this thing with me. I've got nobody to
talk to, Ben, and the woman has suffered, you hear
me?

BEN *(standing still, considering)*. What's the proposition?

WILLY. It's twenty thousand dollars on the barrelhead.
Guaranteed, gilt-edged, you understand?

BEN. You don't want to make a fool of yourself. They
might not honor the policy.

WILLY. How can they dare refuse? Didn't I work like a

---

4 **lettuce:** Kopfsalat.
15f. **the ins and outs:** die Feinheiten; das Für und Wider.
21 **on the barrelhead:** (fig.) auf den Tisch des Hauses, auf die Hand
   (barrelhead: Faßdeckel).
22 **gilt-edged** (coll.): mit Goldschnitt versehen; hier (fig.): erstklassig,
   prima.
24 **to honor the policy:** die Versicherungspolice anerkennen; hier: die
   Versicherungssumme auszahlen.

coolie to meet every premium on the nose? And now
they don't pay off! Impossible!

BEN. It's called a cowardly thing, William.

WILLY. Why? Does it take more guts to stand here the
rest of my life ringing up a zero?

BEN *(yielding).* That's a point, William. *(He moves,
thinking, turns.)* And twenty thousand – that *is* something one can feel with the hand, it is there.

WILLY *(now assured, with rising power).* Oh, Ben, that's
the whole beauty of it! I see it like a diamond, shining
in the dark, hard and rough, that I can pick up and
touch in my hand. Not like – like an appointment!
This would not be another damned-fool appointment, Ben, and it changes all the aspects. Because he
thinks I'm nothing, see, and so he spites me. But the
funeral – *(Straightening up)* – Ben, that funeral
will be massive! They'll come from Maine,
Massachusetts, Vermont, New Hampshire! All the
old-timers with the strange license plates – that boy
will be thunder-struck, Ben, because he never
realized – I am known! Rhode Island, New York,
New Jersey – I am known, Ben, and he'll see it with
his eyes once and for all. He'll see what I am, Ben!
He's in for a shock, that boy!

---

1 **coolie:** Kuli, Tagelöhner.
  to meet a premium on the nose: die Versicherungsprämie pünktlich
  zahlen.
4 **guts** (pl.): Eingeweide; hier (fig.): Mut, Mumm.
5 **to ring up a zero:** kein Geld einnehmen; nichts in der Kasse haben.
6 **yielding:** nachgiebig.
19 **license plate:** Nummernschild (eines Fahrzeugs).
20 **thunder-struck:** wie vom Donner gerührt.
24 **he's in for a shock:** auf den wartet eine Überraschung.

BEN *(coming down to the edge of the garden)*. He'll call you a coward.

WILLY *(suddenly fearful)*. No, that would be terrible.

BEN. Yes. And a damned fool.

WILLY. No, no, he mustn't, I won't have that! *(He is broken and desperate.)*

BEN. He'll hate you, William.

(The gay music of the Boys is heard.)

WILLY. Oh, Ben, how do we get back to all the great times? Used to be so full of light, and comradeship, the sleigh-riding in winter, and the ruddiness on his cheeks. And always some kind of good news coming up, always something nice coming up ahead. And never even let me carry the valises in the house, and simonizing, simonizing that little red car! Why, why can't I give him something and not have him hate me?

BEN. Let me think about it. *(He glances at his watch.)* I still have a little time. Remarkable proposition, but you've got to be sure you're not making a fool of yourself.

(Ben drifts off upstage and goes out of sight. Biff comes down from the left.)

WILLY *(suddenly conscious of Biff, turns and looks up at him, then begins picking up the packages of seeds in confusion)*. Where the hell is that seed? *(Indignantly.)* You can't see nothing out here! They boxed in the whole goddam neighborhood!

BIFF. There are people all around here. Don't you realize that?

WILLY. I'm busy. Don't bother me.

---

11 **sleigh-riding:** Schlittenfahren.
ruddiness: gesunde Röte.

BIFF *(taking the hoe from Willy).* I'm saying good-by to
you, Pop. *(Willy looks at him, silent, unable to move.)*
I'm not coming back any more.

WILLY. You're not going to see Oliver tomorrow?

5 BIFF. I've got no appointment, Dad.

WILLY. He put his arm around you, and you've got no
appointment?

BIFF. Pop, get this now, will you? Everytime I've left it's
been a fight that sent me out of here. Today I realized

10 something about myself and I tried to explain it to
you and I – I think I'm just not smart enough to make
any sense out of it for you. To hell with whose fault it
is or anything like that. *(He takes Willy's arm.)* Let's
just wrap it up, heh? Come on in, we'll tell Mom. *(He*

15 *gently tries to pull Willy to left.)*

WILLY *(frozen, immobile, with guilt in his voice).* No, I
don't want to see her.

BIFF. Come on! *(He pulls again, and Willy tries to pull
away.)*

20 WILLY *(highly nervous).* No, no, I don't want to see her.

BIFF *(tries to look into Willy's face, as if to find the
answer there).* Why don't you want to see her?

WILLY *(more harshly now).* Don't bother me, will you?

BIFF. What do you mean, you don't want to see her?

25 You don't want them calling you yellow, do you?
This isn't your fault; it's me, I'm a bum. Now come
inside! *(Willy strains to get away.)* Did you hear what
I said to you?

(Willy pulls away and quickly goes by himself into the

30 *house. Biff follows.)*

---

13 f. **let's just wrap it up:** laß uns damit Schluß machen.
23 **harshly** (adv.): rauh, barsch.
25 **yellow** (coll.): feige.

LINDA *(to Willy)*. Did you plant, dear?

BIFF *(at the door, to Linda)*. All right, we had it out. I'm going and I'm not writing any more.

LINDA *(going to Willy in the kitchen)*. I think that's the best way, dear. 'Cause there's no use drawing it out, you'll just never get along.
(Willy doesn't respond.)

BIFF. People ask where I am and what I'm doing, you don't know, and you don't care. That way it'll be off your mind and you can start brightening up again. All right? That clears it, doesn't it? *(Willy is silent, and Biff goes to him.)* You gonna wish me luck, scout? *(He extends his hand.)* What do you say?

LINDA. Shake his hand, Willy.

WILLY *(turning to her, seething with hurt)*. There's no necessity to mention the pen at all, y'know.

BIFF *(gently)*. I've got no appointment, Dad.

WILLY *(erupting fiercely)*. He put his arm around . . .?

BIFF. Dad, you're never going to see what I am, so what's the use of arguing? If I strike oil I'll send you a check. Meantime forget I'm alive.

WILLY *(to Linda)*. Spite, see?

BIFF. Shake hands, Dad.

WILLY. Not my hand.

BIFF. I was hoping not to go this way.

WILLY. Well, this is the way you're going. Good-by.
(Biff looks at him a moment, then turns sharply and goes to the stairs.)

WILLY *(stops him with)*. May you rot in hell if you leave this house!

BIFF *(turning)*. Exactly what is it that you want from me?

---

15 **seething with hurt:** vom Schmerz überwältigt.
18 **to erupt:** ausbrechen.

WILLY. I want you to know, on the train, in the mountains, in the valleys, wherever you go, that you cut
down your life for spite!

BIFF. No, no.

5 WILLY. Spite, spite, is the word of your undoing! And
when you're down and out, remember what did it.
When you're rotting somewhere beside the railroad
tracks, remember, and don't you dare blame it on
me!

10 BIFF. I'm not blaming it on you!

WILLY. I won't take the rap for this, you hear?
*(Happy comes down the stairs and stands on the
bottom step, watching.)*

BIFF. That's just what I'm telling you!

15 WILLY *(sinking into a chair at the table, with full accusa-
tion)*. You're trying to put a knife in me – don't think
I don't know what you're doing!

BIFF. All right, phony! Then let's lay it on the line. *(He
whips the rubber tube out of his pocket and puts it on
20   the table.)*

HAPPY. You crazy –

LINDA. Biff! *(She moves to grab the hose, but Biff holds it
down with his hand.)*

BIFF. Leave it there! Don't move it!

25 WILLY *(not looking at it)*. What is that?

BIFF. You know goddam well what that is.

WILLY *(caged, wanting to escape)*. I never saw that.

---

5 **undoing:** Vernichtung, Zerstörung; Unglück.
6 **to be down and out:** fix und fertig sein.
11 **to take the rap** (coll.): die Schuld auf sich nehmen.
18 **to lay it on the line:** etwas unverblümt offenlegen; mit etwas raus-
rücken.
27 **caged:** ertappt; in die Enge getrieben.

BIFF. You saw it. The mice didn't bring it into the cellar! What is this supposed to do, make a hero out of you? This supposed to make me sorry for you?

WILLY. Never heard of it.

5 BIFF. There'll be no pity for you, you hear it? No pity!

WILLY *(to Linda)*. You hear the spite!

BIFF. No, you're going to hear the truth – what you are and what I am!

LINDA. Stop it!

10 WILLY. Spite!

HAPPY *(coming down toward Biff)*. You cut it now!

BIFF *(to Happy)*. The man don't know who we are! The man is gonna know! *(To Willy.)* We never told the truth for ten minutes in this house!

15 HAPPY. We always told the truth!

BIFF *(turning on him)*. You big blow, are you the assistant buyer? You're one of the two assistants to the assistant, aren't you?

HAPPY. Well, I'm practically –

20 BIFF. You're practically full of it! We all are! And I'm through with it. *(To Willy.)* Now hear this, Willy, this is me.

WILLY. I know you!

BIFF. You know why I had no address for three months? I
25 stole a suit in Kansas City and I was in jail. *(To Linda, who is sobbing.)* Stop crying. I'm through with it. *(Linda turns away from them, her hands covering her face.)*

WILLY. I suppose that's my fault!

30 BIFF. I stole myself out of every good job since high school!

16 **big blow** (slang): Angeber, ›großes Tier‹.

WILLY. And whose fault is that?

BIFF. And I never got anywhere because you blew me so full of hot air I could never stand taking orders from anybody! That's whose fault it is!

5 WILLY. I hear that!

LINDA. Don't, Biff!

BIFF. It's goddam time you heard that! I had to be boss big shot in two weeks, and I'm through with it!

WILLY. Then hang yourself! For spite, hang yourself!

10 BIFF. No! Nobody's hanging himself, Willy! I ran down eleven flights with a pen in my hand today. And suddenly I stopped, you hear me? And in the middle of that office building, do you hear this? I stopped in the middle of that building and I saw – the sky. I saw

15 the things that I love in this world. The work and the food and time to sit and smoke. And I looked at the pen and said to myself, what the hell am I grabbing this for? Why am I trying to become what I don't want to be? What am I doing in an office, making a

20 contemptuous, begging fool of myself, when all I want is out there, waiting for me the minute I say I know who I am! Why can't I say that, Willy? *(He tries to make Willy face him, but Willy pulls away and moves to the left.)*

25 WILLY *(with hatred, threateningly)*. The door of your life is wide open!

BIFF. Pop! I'm a dime a dozen, and so are you!

WILLY *(turning on him now in an uncontrolled outburst).*

---

2 f. **to blow s.o. full of hot air:** jdn. aufgeblasen machen; jdm. Flausen in den Kopf setzen.

20 **contemptuous:** verächtlich.

27 **a dime a dozen:** Dutzendware.

I am not a dime a dozen! I am Willy Loman, and you
are Biff Loman!

*(Biff starts for Willy, but is blocked by Happy. In his
fury, Biff seems on the verge of attacking his father.)*

BIFF. I am not a leader of men, Willy, and neither are
you. You were never anything but a hard-working
drummer who landed in the ash can like all the rest of
them! I'm one dollar an hour, Willy! I tried seven
states and couldn't raise it. A buck an hour! Do you
gather my meaning? I'm not bringing home any
prizes any more, and you're going to stop waiting for
me to bring them home!

WILLY *(directly to Biff).* You vengeful, spiteful mut!

*(Biff breaks from Happy. Willy, in fright, starts up the
stairs. Biff graps him.)*

BIFF *(at the peak of his fury).* Pop, I'm nothing! I'm
nothing, Pop. Can't you understand that? There's no
spite in it any more. I'm just what I am, that's all.

*(Biff's fury has spent itself, and he breaks down,
sobbing, holding on to Willy, who dumbly fumbles for
Biff's face.)*

WILLY *(astonished).* What're you doing? What're you
doing? *(To Linda.)* Why is he crying?

BIFF *(crying, broken).* Will you let me go, for Christ's
sake? Will you take that phony dream and burn it
before something happens? *(Struggling to contain
himself, he pulls away and moves to the stairs.)* I'll

---

13 **vengeful:** rachsüchtig.
   mut (slang): Köter, Bastard.
16 **at the peak:** auf dem Höhepunkt.
20 **to fumble:** umhertasten.
26f. **to contain o.s.:** sich zusammennehmen, sich fassen.

go in the morning. Put him – put him to bed.
(Exhausted, Biff moves up the stairs to his room.)

WILLY *(after a long pause, astonished, elevated)*. Isn't
that – isn't that remarkable? Biff – he likes me!

5 LINDA. He loves you, Willy!

HAPPY *(deeply moved)*. Always did, Pop.

WILLY. Oh, Biff! *(Staring wildly.)* He cried! Cried to me.
*(He is choking with his love, and now cries out his
promise.)* That boy – that boy is going to be magnifi-

10   cent!

(Ben appears in the light just outside the kitchen.)

BEN. Yes, outstanding, with twenty thousand behind
him.

LINDA *(sensing the racing of his mind, fearfully, care-*

15   *fully)*. Now come to bed, Willy. It's all settled now.

WILLY *(finding it difficult not to rush out of the house)*.
Yes, we'll sleep. Come on. Go to sleep, Hap.

BEN. And it does take a great kind of a man to crack the
jungle.

20   *(In accents of dread, Ben's idyllic music starts up.)*

HAPPY *(his arm around Linda)*. I'm getting married,
Pop, don't forget it. I'm changing everything. I'm
gonna run that department before the year is up.
You'll see, Mom. *(He kisses her.)*

25 BEN. The jungle is dark but full of diamonds, Willy.
(Willy turns, moves, listening to Ben.)

LINDA. Be good. You're both good boys, just act that
way, that's all.

HAPPY. 'Night, Pop. *(He goes upstairs.)*

30 LINDA *(to Willy)*. Come, dear.

---

3 **elevated:** aufgemuntert; in gehobener Stimmung.
20 **in accents of dread:** mit bedrohlichem Unterton.

BEN *(with greater force).* One must go in to fetch a
diamond out.

WILLY *(to Linda, as he moves slowly along the edge of
the kitchen, toward the door).* I just want to get
settled down, Linda. Let me sit alone for a little.

LINDA *(almost uttering her fear).* I want you upstairs.

WILLY *(taking her in his arms).* In a few minutes, Linda.
I couldn't sleep right now. Go on, you look awful
tired. *(He kisses her.)*

BEN. Not like an appointment at all. A diamond is rough
and hard to the touch.

WILLY. Go on now. I'll be right up.

LINDA. I think this is the only way, Willy.

WILLY. Sure, it's the best thing.

BEN. Best thing!

WILLY. The only way. Everything is gonna be – go on,
kid, get to bed. You look so tired.

LINDA. Come right up.

WILLY. Two minutes.

*(Linda goes into the living-room, then reappears in
her bedroom. Willy moves just outside the kitchen
door.)*

WILLY. Loves me. *(Wonderingly.)* Always loved me.
Isn't that a remarkable thing? Ben, he'll worship me
for it!

BEN *(with promise).* It's dark there, but full of
diamonds.

WILLY. Can you imagine that magnificence with twenty
thousand dollars in his pocket?

LINDA *(calling from her room).* Willy! Come up!

WILLY *(calling into the kitchen).* Yes! Yes. Coming! It's

---

28 **magnificence:** Herrlichkeit; hier: herrliches Gefühl.

very smart, you realize that, don't you, sweetheart?
Even Ben sees it. I gotta go, baby. 'By! 'By! (*Going
over to Ben, almost dancing.*) Imagine? When the
mail comes he'll be ahead of Bernard again!

5 BEN. A perfect proposition all around.

WILLY. Did you see how he cried to me? Oh, if I could
kiss him, Ben!

BEN. Time, William, time!

WILLY. Oh, Ben, I always knew one way or another we
10   were gonna make it, Biff and I!

BEN (*looking at his watch*). The boat. We'll be late. (*He
moves slowly off into the darkness.*)

WILLY (*elegiacally, turning to the house*). Now when you
kick off, boy, I want a seventy-yard boot, and get
15   right down the field under the ball, and when you hit,
hit low and hit hard, because it's important, boy. (*He
swings around and faces the audience.*) There's all
kinds of important people in the stands, and the first
thing you know . . . (*Suddenly realizing he is alone.*)
20   Ben! Ben, where do I . . .? (*He makes a sudden
movement of search.*) Ben, how do I . . .?

LINDA (*calling*). Willy, you coming up?

WILLY (*uttering a gasp of fear, whirling about as if to
quiet her*). Sh! (*He turns around as if to find his way;
25   sounds, faces, voices, seem to be swarming in upon
him and he flicks at them, crying, Sh! Sh! Suddenly
music, faint and high, stops him. It rises in intensity,
almost to an unbearable scream. He goes up and*

---

13 **elegiacally** (*adv.*): elegisch, wehmütig.
14 **to kick off** (Am. football): zur Spieleröffnung anstoßen.
   boot: hier: Schuß.
18 **stand:** Tribüne.
26 **to flick at s.th.:** nach etwas schlagen.

down on his toes, and rushes off around the house.)
Shhh!

LINDA. Willy?

(There is no answer. Linda waits. Biff gets up off his
5 *bed. He is still in his clothes. Happy sits up. Biff stands*
listening.)

LINDA *(with real fear).* Willy, answer me! Willy!

(There is the sound of a car starting and moving away
at full speed.)

10 LINDA. No!

BIFF *(rushing down the stairs).* Pop!

(As the car speeds off, the music crashes down in a
frenzy of sound, which becomes the soft pulsation of a
single cello string. Biff slowly returns to his bedroom.
15 *He and Happy gravely don their jackets. Linda slowly*
walks out of her room. The music has developed into a
dead march. The leaves of day are appearing over
everything. Charley and Bernard, somberly dressed,
appear and knock on the kitchen door. Biff and
20 *Happy slowly descend the stairs to the kitchen as*
Charley and Bernard enter. All stop a moment when
Linda, in clothes of mourning, bearing a little bunch
of roses, comes through the draped doorway into the
kitchen. She goes to Charley and takes his arm. Now
25 *all move toward the audience, through the wall-line of*
the kitchen. At the limit of the apron, Linda lays down
the flowers, kneels, and sits back on her heels. All
stare down at the grave.)

---

15 **to don:** anziehen.
18 **somberly** (adv.): dunkel.
22 **clothes of mourning:** Trauerkleidung.

Requiem

CHARLEY. It's getting dark, Linda.
(Linda doesn't react. She stares at the grave.)

BIFF. How about it, Mom? Better get some rest, heh?
5 They'll be closing the gate soon.
(Linda makes no move. Pause.)

HAPPY *(deeply angered)*. He had no right to do that.
There was no necessity for it. We would've helped
him.

10 CHARLEY *(grunting)*. Hmmm.

BIFF. Come along, Mom.

LINDA. Why didn't anybody come?

CHARLEY. It was a very nice funeral.

LINDA. But where are all the people he knew? Maybe
15 they blame him.

CHARLEY. Naa. It's a rough world, Linda. They wouldn't
blame him.

LINDA. I can't understand it. At this time especially.
First time in thirty-five years we were just about free
20 and clear. He only needed a little salary. He was even
finished with the dentist.

CHARLEY. No man only needs a little salary.

LINDA. I can't understand it.

BIFF. There were a lot of nice days. When he'd come
25 home from a trip; or on Sundays, making the stoop;

---

10 **to grunt:** brummen.

finishing the cellar; putting on the new porch; when
he built the extra bathroom; and put up the garage.
You know something, Charley, there's more of him
in that front stoop than in all the sales he ever made.

5 CHARLEY. Yeah. He was a happy man with a batch of
cement.

LINDA. He was so wonderful with his hands.

BIFF. He had the wrong dreams. All, all, wrong.

HAPPY *(almost ready to fight Biff)*. Don't say that!

10 BIFF. He never knew who he was.

CHARLEY *(stopping Happy's movement and reply. To
Biff)*. Nobody dast blame this man. You don't understand: Willy was a salesman. And for a salesman,
there is no rock bottom to the life. He don't put a bolt

15 to a nut, he don't tell you the law or give you
medicine. He's a man way out there in the blue,
riding on a smile and a shoeshine. And when they
start not smiling back – that's an earthquake. And
then you get yourself a couple of spots on your hat,

20 and you're finished. Nobody dast blame this man. A
salesman is got to dream, boy. It comes with the
territory.

BIFF. Charley, the man didn't know who he was.

HAPPY *(infuriated)*. Don't say that!

25 BIFF. Why don't you come with me, Happy?

---

1 **porch:** überdachter Hauseingang; Veranda.
5f. **batch of cement:** etwa: ein Sack Zement.
12 **dast** (slang): *dare*.
14 **rock bottom:** Tiefpunkt.
14f. **to put a bolt to a nut:** mit Schrauben und Muttern hantieren; (fig.)
    handwerklich arbeiten.
18 **earthquake:** Erdbeben.
24 **infuriated:** wütend.

HAPPY. I'm not licked that easily. I'm staying right in this
city, and I'm gonna beat this racket! *(He looks at Biff,
his chin set.)* The Loman Brothers!

BIFF. I know who I am, kid.

5 HAPPY. All right, boy. I'm gonna show you and everybody else that Willy Loman did not die in vain. He
had a good dream. It's the only dream you can have –
to come out number-one man. He fought it out here,
and this is where I'm gonna win it for him.

10 BIFF *(with a hopeless glance at Happy, bends toward his
mother)*. Let's go, Mom.

LINDA. I'll be with you in a minute. Go on, Charley. *(He
hesitates.)* I want to, just for a minute. I never had a
chance to say good-by.

15 *(Charley moves away, followed by Happy. Biff
remains a slight distance up and left of Linda. She sits
there, summoning herself. The flute begins, not far
away, playing behind her speech.)*

LINDA. Forgive me, dear. I can't cry. I don't know what it
20 is, but I can't cry. I don't understand it. Why did you
ever do that? Help me, Willy, I can't cry. It seems to me
that you're just on another trip. I keep expecting you.
Willy, dear, I can't cry. Why did you do it? I search and
search and I search, and I can't understand it, Willy. I
25 made the last payment on the house today. Today,
dear. And there'll be nobody home. *(A sob rises in her
throat.)* We're free and clear. *(Sobbing more fully,
released.)* We're free. *(Biff comes slowly toward her.)*
We're free ... We're free ...

---

1 **to be licked** (coll.): sich geschlagen geben, sich unterkriegen lassen.
2 **racket** (coll.): Bande, verschworener Haufen.
17 **to summon o.s.:** sich sammeln.

(Biff lifts her to her feet and moves out up right with her in his arms. Linda sobs quietly. Bernard and Charley come together and follow them, followed by Happy. Only the music of the flute is left on the darkening stage as over the house the hard towers of the apartment buildings rise into sharp focus.)

6 **to rise into sharp focus:** in den Brennpunkt treten; deutlich sichtbar werden.

Editorische Notiz

Der englische Text folgt der Ausgabe: Arthur Miller, *Collected Plays*, New York: Viking Press, 1957. Das Glossar erklärt in der Regel alle Wörter, die über die Wertigkeitsstufe 4 des *Englischen Arbeitswörterbuches* von Alfred Haase (Frankfurt a. M.: Moritz Diesterweg, ⁷1979) hinausgehen. Im Zweifelsfall wurde großzügig verfahren, d. h. eher eine Vokabel mehr aufgenommen als dort vorgesehen.

Im Glossar verwendete Abkürzungen

adv.	adverb
AE	American English
Am.	American
arch.	archaic (veraltet)
coll.	colloquial (umgangssprachlich)
fig.	figuratively (übertragen)
frz.	französisch
ital.	italienisch
milit.	military (Militärsprache)
o.s.	oneself
pl.	plural
s.o.	someone
s.th.	something
vulg.	vulgar (vulgär, derb)

Auswahlbibliographie

Bibliographien

Eissenstat, Martha Turnquist, »Arthur Miller: A Bibliography«, in: *Modern Drama* 5 (1962/63) S. 93–106.

Ferres, John H., *Arthur Miller: A Reference Guide*, Boston 1979.

Hayashi, Tetsumaro, *An Index to Arthur Miller Criticism*, Metuchen, N. J., 1976.

Ungar, Harriet, »The Writings of and about Arthur Miller: A Check List 1936–1967«, in: *Bulletin of the New York Public Library* 74 (1970) S. 107–134.

Monographien, kritische Studien, Rezensionen

Adamczewski, Zygmunt, »The Tragic Loss – Loman the Salesman«, in: Z. A., *The Tragic Protest*, Den Haag 1963, S. 172–192.

Angélico da Costa, Luiz, »The Role of Language in *Death of a Salesman*«, in: *Estudos Anglo-Americanos* 2 (1978) S. 21–31.

Barksdale, Richard K., »Social Background in the Plays of Miller and Williams«, in: *CLA Journal* 6 (1963) S. 161–169.

Bates, Barclay W., »The Lost Past in *Death of a Salesman*«, in: *Modern Drama* 11 (1968/69) S. 164–172.

Bettina, Sister M., »Willy Loman's Brother Ben: Tragic Insight in *Death of a Salesman*«, in: *Modern Drama* 4 (1961/62) S. 409–412.

Bierman, Judah/Hart, James/Johnson, Stanley, »Arthur Miller: *Death of a Salesman*«, in: J. B. / J. H. / St. J. *The Dramatic Experience*, Englewood Cliffs, N. J., 1958, S. 490–493.

Bliquez, Guerin, »Linda's Role in *Death of a Salesman*«, in: *Modern Drama* 10 (1967/68) S. 383–386.

Bock, Hedwig, »Die Rolle der Frau in Arthur Millers frühen Dramen. Untersuchungen zu seinem Konzept gesellschaftlicher Wirklichkeit«, in: *Literarische Ansichten der Wirklich-keit*, hrsg. von H.-H. Freitag und P. Hühn, Frankfurt a. M. 1980, S. 307–322.

Carson, Neil, *Arthur Miller*, London 1982.

Clark, Eleanor, »Old Glamour, New Gloom«, in: *Partisan Review* 16 (1949) S. 631–636.

Coffin, Rachel W. (Hrsg.), »*Death of a Salesman*«, in: *New York Theatre Critics' Reviews* 10 (1949) S. 358–361.

Cook, Larry W., »The Function of Ben and Dave Singleman in *Death of a Salesman*«, in: *Notes on Contemporary Literature* 5 (1975) S. 7–9.

Corrigan, Robert W. (Hrsg.), *Arthur Miller: A Collection of Critical Essays*, Englewood Cliffs, N. J., 1969.

Couchman, Gordon W., »Arthur Miller's Tragedy of Babbitt«, in: *Educational Theatre Journal* 7 (1955) S. 206–211.

Driver, Tom F., »Strength and Weakness in Arthur Miller«, in: *Tulane Drama Review* 4 (1960) S. 105–113.

Eisinger, Chester E., »Focus on Arthur Miller's *Death of a Salesman*: The Wrong Dreams«, in: *American Dreams, American Nightmares*, hrsg. von David Madden, Carbondale 1970, S. 165–174.

Ferguson, Alfred R., »The Tragedy of the American Dream in *Death of a Salesman*«, in: *Thought* 53 (1978) S. 83–98.

Field, B. S., »*Death of a Salesman*«, in: *Twentieth Century Literature* 18 (1972) S. 19–24.

Gardner, R. H., »Tragedy of the Lowest Man«, in: R. H. G., *The Splintered Stage*, New York 1965, S. 122–134.

Gassner, John, »*Death of a Salesman*: First Impressions, 1949«, in: J. G., *The Theatre in Our Times*, New York 1954, S. 364–373.

Goetsch, Paul, »Arthur Millers Zeitkritik in *Death of a Salesman*«, in: *Die Neueren Sprachen* N. F. 16 (1967) S. 105–117.

– »Arthur Miller: *Death of a Salesman*«, in: *Das amerikanische Drama*, hrsg. von P. Goetsch, Düsseldorf 1974, S. 208–233.

Grandel, Hartmut, »*Death of a Salesman* – Tragödie oder

soziales Drama?«, in: *Amerikanisches Drama und Theater im 20. Jahrhundert*, hrsg. von A. Weber und S. Neuweiler, Göttingen 1975, S. 204–222.

Groene, Horst, »*Death of a Salesman* – Beispielhafte amerikanische Dramenkunst«, in: *Literatur in Wissenschaft und Unterricht* 4 (1971) S. 177–186.

Gross, Barry E., »Peddler and Pioneer in *Death of a Salesman*«, in: *Modern Drama* 7 (1964/65) S. 405–410.

Gupta, R. K., »*Death of a Salesman* and Miller's Concept of Tragedy«, in: *Kyushu American Literature* 15 (1974) S. 10–19.

Hagopian, John V., »*Death of a Salesman*«, in: *Insight I*, hrsg. von J. V. H. und M. Dolch, Frankfurt a. M. 1962, S. 174–186.

– »Arthur Miller: The Salesman's Two Cases«, in: *Modern Drama* 6 (1963/64) S. 117–125.

Hallett, Charles A., »The Retrospective Technique and Its Implications for Tragedy«, in: *Comparative Drama* 12 (1978) S. 3–22.

Harshbarger, Karl, *The Burning Jungle: An Analysis of Arthur Miller's »Death of a Salesman«*, Washington, D. C., 1977.

Hayman, Ronald, *Arthur Miller*, New York 1972.

Heilman, Robert B., »Salesmen's Deaths: Documentary and Myth«, in: *Shenandoah* 20 (1969) S. 20–28.

Heyen, William, »Arthur Miller's *Death of a Salesman* and the American Dream«, in: *Amerikanisches Drama und Theater im 20. Jahrhundert*, hrsg. von A. Weber und S. Neuweiler, Göttingen 1975, S. 190–203.

Hoeveler, D. L., »*Death of a Salesman* as Psychomachia«, in: *Journal of American Culture* 1 (1978) S. 632–637.

Huftel, Sheila, *Arthur Miller: The Burning Glass*, New York 1965.

Hurrell, John D. (Hrsg.), *Two Modern American Tragedies: Reviews and Criticism of »Death of a Salesman« and »A Streetcar Named Desire«*, New York 1961.

Hynes, Joseph A., »Attention Must Be Paid . . .«, in: *College English* 23 (1962) S. 574–578.

Hynes, Joseph A., »Arthur Miller and the Impasse of Naturalism«, in: *South Atlantic Quarterly* 62 (1963) S. 327–334.

Jackson, Esther Merle, »*Death of a Salesman*: Tragic Myth in the Modern Theatre«, in: *CLA Journal* 7 (1963) S. 63–76.

Jacobson, Irving, »Family Dreams in *Death of a Salesman*«, in: *American Literature* 47 (1975) S. 247–258.

James, Stuart B., »Pastoral Dreamer in an Urban World«, in: *University of Denver Quarterly* 1 (1966) S. 45–57.

Jochems, Helmut, »*Death of a Salesman* – Eine Nachlese«, in: *Literatur in Wissenschaft und Unterricht* 1 (1968) S. 77–97.

Kennedy, Sighle, »Who Killed the Salesman?«, in: *Catholic World* 170 (1970) S. 110–116.

Kernodle, George R., »The Death of the Little Man«, in: *The Carleton Drama Review* 1 (1955/56) S. 47–60.

Köhler, Klaus, »Bewußtseinsanalyse und Gesellschaftskrise im Dramenwerk Arthur Millers«, in: *Zeitschrift für Anglistik und Amerikanistik* 22 (1974) S. 18–40.

Koon, Helene Wickham (Hrsg.), *Twentieth Century Interpretations of »Death of a Salesman«: A Collection of Critical Essays*, Englewood Cliffs, N. J., 1983.

Lawrence, Stephen A., »The Right Dream in Miller's *Death of a Salesman*«, in: *College English* 25 (1963/64) S. 547–549.

Mander, John, »Arthur Miller's *Death of a Salesman*«, in: J. M., *The Writer and Commitment*, London 1961, S. 138–152.

Manocchio, Tony / Roberts, Patrick, »The Loman Family«, in: T. M. / P. R., *Families Under Stress: A Psychological Interpretation*, Boston 1975, S. 129–168.

Martin, Robert A. (Hrsg.), *Arthur Miller: New Perspectives*, Englewood Cliffs, N. J., 1982.

Martine, James J. (Hrsg.), *Critical Essays on Arthur Miller*, Boston 1979.

McAnany, Emile G., »The Tragic Commitment: Some Notes on Arthur Miller«, in: *Modern Drama* 5 (1962/63) S. 11–20.

McMahon, Helen M., »Arthur Miller's Common Man: The Problem of Realistic and Mythic«, in: *Drama and Theatre* 10 (1972) S. 128–133.

Mielziner, Jo, »Designing a Play: *Death of a Salesman*«, in: J. M., *Designing for the Theatre*, New York 1965, S. 23–63.

Miller, Arthur, *Timebends*, New York 1987.

Miller, Arthur [u. a.], »*Death of a Salesman*: A Symposium«, in: *Tulane Drama Review* 2 (1958) S. 63–69.

Miller, Jordan Y., »Myth and the American Dream: O'Neill to Albee«, in: *Modern Drama* 7 (1964/65) S. 190–198.

Moss, Leonard, *Arthur Miller*, New York 1967, rev. Aufl. Boston 1980.

– »*Death of a Salesman*: Verbal and Symbolic Technique«, in: *Das amerikanische Drama von den Anfängen bis zur Gegenwart*, hrsg. von Hans Itschert, Darmstadt 1972, S. 378–384.

Mottram, Eric, »Arthur Miller: the Development of a Political Dramatist in America«, in: *American Theatre*, London 1967 (Stratford-upon-Avon Studies, 10), S. 127–161.

Murray, Edward, *Arthur Miller, Dramatist*, New York 1967.

Nelson, Benjamin, *Arthur Miller: Portrait of a Playwright*, New York 1970.

Oberg, Arthur K., »*Death of a Salesman* and Arthur Miller's Search for Style«, in: *Criticism* 9 (1967) S. 303–311.

Otten, Charlotte F., »Who am I? ... A Re-Investigation of Arthur Miller's *Death of a Salesman*«, in: *Cresset* 26 (1963) S. 11–13.

Parker, Brian, »Point of View in Arthur Miller's *Death of a Salesman*«, in: *University of Toronto Quarterly* 35 (1966) S. 144–157.

Popkin, Henry, »Arthur Miller: The Strange Encounter«, in: *Sewanee Review* 68 (1960) S. 34–60.

Prudhoe, John, »Arthur Miller and the Tradition of Tragedy«, in: *English Studies* 43 (1962) S. 430–439.

Ranald, Margaret Loftus, »*Death of a Salesman*: Fifteen Years After«, in: *Comment: A New Zealand Quarterly* 6 (1965) S. 28–35.

Razum, Hannes, »Schuld und Verantwortung im Werk Arthur Millers«, in: *Theater und Drama in Amerika*, hrsg. von E. Lohner und R. Haas, Berlin 1978, S. 310–320.

Rössle, Wolfgang, *Die soziale Wirklichkeit in Arthur Millers »Death of a Salesman«*, Freiburg (Schweiz) 1970.

Saisselin, Rémy G., »Is Tragic Drama Possible in the Twentieth Century?«, in: *The Theatre Annual* 17 (1960) S. 12–21.

Schäfer, Jürgen, »Arthur Miller«, in: J. Sch., *Geschichte des amerikanischen Dramas im 20. Jahrhundert*, Stuttgart 1982, S. 115–123.

Schweinitz, George de, »*Death of a Salesman:* A Note on Epic and Tragedy«, in: *Western Humanities Review* 14 (1960) S. 91–96.

Shatzky, Joel, »The ›Reactive Image‹ and Miller's *Death of a Salesman*«, in: *Players Magazine* 48 (1973) S. 104–110.

Shaw, Patrick W., »The Ironic Characterization of Bernard in *Death of a Salesman*«, in: *Notes on Contemporary Literature* 11 (1981) S. 12.

Shelton, Frank W., »Sports and the Competitive Ethic: *Death of a Salesman* and *That Championship Season*«, in: *Ball State University Forum* 20 (1979) S. 17–21.

Siegel, Paul N., »Willy Loman and King Lear«, in: *College English* 17 (1956) S. 341–345.

Steinberg, M. W., »Arthur Miller and the Ideas of Modern Tragedy«, in: *Dalhousie Review* 40 (1960) S. 329–340.

Trowbridge, Clinton, »Arthur Miller: Between Pathos and Tragedy«, in: *Modern Drama* 10 (1967/68) S. 221–232.

Vogel, Dan, »Willy Tyrannos«, in: D. V., *The Three Masks of American Tragedy*, Baton Rouge, La., 1974, S. 91–102.

Weales, Gerald C. (Hrsg.), *Arthur Miller: »Death of a Salesman«, Text and Criticism*, New York 1967. [Neben einer Textausgabe bietet dieses Buch die bisher umfangreichste Anthologie von Rezensionen und Artikeln zu dem Drama.]

Welland, Dennis, *Miller: A Study of His Plays*, London [3]1985.

Wells, Arvin R., »Arthur Miller: the Dramatist as Social Critic?«, in: *Das amerikanische Drama von den Anfängen bis zur Gegenwart*, hrsg. von Hans Itschert, Darmstadt 1972, S. 353–366.

Whitley, Alvin, »Arthur Miller: An Attempt at Modern Tragedy«, in: *Transactions of the Wisconsin Academy of Sciences, Arts and Letters* 42 (1953) S. 257–262.

Williams, Raymond, »The Realism of Arthur Miller«, in: *Critical Quarterly* 1 (1959) S. 140–149.

Wilson, Robert N., »Arthur Miller: The Salesman and Society«, in: R. N. W., *The Writer as Social Seer*, Chapel Hill 1979, S. 56–71.

Nachtrag 1985–2000

Abbotson, Susan C. W., *Student Companion to Arthur Miller*, Westport, CT, 2000.

Ardolino, Frank, »Miller's Use of Demotic English in *Death of a Salesman*«, in: *Studies in American Jewish Literature* 17 (1998) S. 120–128.

August, Eugene R., »*Death of a Salesman*: A Men's Studies Approach«, in: *Western Ohio Journal* 7.1 (1986) S. 53–71.

Austin, Gayle, »Arthur Miller's *Death of a Salesman*«, in: *Feminist Theories for Dramatic Criticism*, Ann Arbor, MI, 1990, S. 47–51.

Babcock, Granger, »What's the Secret?: Willy Loman as Desiring Machine«, in: *American Drama* 2.1 (Fall 1992) S. 59–83.

Balakian, Janet, »Private Tensions Raised to a Poetic-Social Level«, in: *The Achievement of Arthur Miller: New Essays*, hrsg. von Steven R. Centola, Dallas 1995, S. 59–67.

Becker, Benjamin J., »*Death of a Salesman*: Arthur Miller's Play in the Light of Psychoanalysis«, in: *American Journal of Psychoanalysis* 47.3 (Fall 1987) S. 195–209.

Bigsby, Christopher (Hrsg.), *The Cambridge Companion to Arthur Miller*, Cambridge 1997.

Bloom, Harold (Hrsg.), *Arthur Miller*, Broomall, PA, 2000.

– (Hrsg.) *Major Literary Characters: Willy Loman*, New York 1990.

– (Hrsg.) *Modern Critical Interpretations: Arthur Miller's »Death of a Salesman«*, New York / Philadelphia 1988.

Bloom, Harold (Hrsg.) *Arthur Miller: Modern Critical Views*, New York / Philadelphia 1987.

Bodmer, George R., »A Sartrean Reading of Arthur Miller's *Death of a Salesman*«, in: *Journal of Evolutionary Psychology* 9 (1988) S. 297–302.

Burgard, Peter J., »Two Parts Ibsen, One Part American Dream: On Derivation and Originality in Arthur Miller's *Death of a Salesman*«, in: *Orbis Litterarum* 43.4 (1988) S. 336–353.

Canning, Charlotte, »Is This a Play About Women? A Feminist Reading of *Death of a Salesman*«, in: *The Achievement of Arthur Miller: New Essays*, hrsg. von Steven R. Centola, Dallas 1995, S. 69–76.

Centola, Steven R., »Family Values in *Death of a Salesman*«, in: *CLA Journal* 37.1 (1993) S. 29–41.

Cook, Kimberly K. »Valentin and Biff: Each Unhappy is His Own Way?«, in: *Journal of Evolutionary Psychology* 16.1 (1995) S. 47–52.

Dukore, Bernard F., *»Death of a Salesman« and »The Crucible«: Text and Performance*, London 1989.

Griffin, Alice, *Understanding Arthur Miller*, Columbia, SC, 1996.

Harder, Harry, »*Death of a Salesman*: An American Classic«, in: *Censored Books: Critical Viewpoints*, hrsg. von N. Karolides, L. Burress, J. M. Kean, Metuchen, N. J., 1993, S. 209–219.

Hark, Ina Rae, »A Frontier Closes in Brooklyn: *Death of a Salesman* and the Turner Thesis«, in: *Postscript* 3 (1986) S. 1–6.

Harris, Andrew, »*Death of a Salesman*«, in: *Broadway Theatre*, New York 1994, S. 48–67.

Kolin, Philip C., »*Death of a Salesman*: A Playwrights' Forum«, in: *Michigan Quarterly Review* 37.4 (Fall 1998) S. 591–623.

Koorey, Stefani, *Arthur Miller's Life and Literature: An Annotated and Comprehensive Guide*, Lanham, MD, 2000.

Krohn, Alan, »The Source of Manhood in *Death of a Sales-*

man«, in: *International Review of Psycho-Analysis* 15 (1988) S. 455–463.

Kullman, Colby H., »*Death of a Salesman* at Fifty: An Interview with Arthur Miller«, in: *Michigan Quarterly Review* 37.4 (Fall 1998) S. 624–634.

Langteau, Paula, »Miller's *Salesman:* An Early Version of Absurdist Theatre«, in: *The Achievement of Arthur Miller: New Essays*, hrsg. von Steven R. Centola, Dallas 1995, S. 77–85.

Marino, Stephen A., *The Salesman Has a Birthday: Essays Celebrating the Fiftieth Anniversary of Arthur Miller's* »*Death of a Salesman*«, Lanham, MD, 2000.

Martin, Robert A., »The Nature of Tragedy in Arthur Miller's *Death of a Salesman*«, in: *South Atlantic Review* 61.4 (Fall 1996) S. 97–106.

Mitchell, Giles, »Living and Dying for the Ideal: A Study of Willy Loman's Narcissism«, in: *Psychoanalytic Review* 77.3 (Fall 1990) S. 391–407.

Murphy, Brenda, »Willy Loman: Icon of Business Culture«, in: *Michigan Quarterly Review* 37.4 (Fall 1998) S. 755–766.

– »Arthur Miller: Revisioning Realism«, in: *Realism and the American Dramatic Tradition*, hrsg. von William W. Demastes, Tuscaloosa/London 1996, S. 189–202.

– »The Reformation of Biff Loman: A View from the Pre-Production Scripts«, in: *The Achievement of Arthur Miller: New Essays*, hrsg. von Steven R. Centola, Dallas 1995, S. 51–57.

– *Miller: Death of a Salesman*, Cambridge 1995.

Murphy, Brenda / Abbotson, Susan C. W., *Understanding* »*Death of a Salesman*«: *A Student Casebook to Issues, Sources, and Historical Documents*, Westport, CT, 1999.

Otten, Terry, »*Death of a Salesman* at Fifty – Still ›Coming Home to Roost‹«, in: *Texas Studies in Literature and Language* 41.3 (Fall 1999) S. 280–310.

Phelps, H. C., »Miller's *Death of a Salesman*«, in: *The Explicator* 53.4 (1995) S. 239–240.

– »The Fat and the Lean Years of Biff and Bernard: An Overlooked Parallelism in *Death of a Salesman*«, in: *Notes on Contemporary Literature* 25.4 (1995) S. 9–11.

Roudané, Matthew C., »*Death of a Salesman* and the Poetics of Arthur Miller«, in: *The Cambridge Companion to Arthur Miller*, hrsg. von Christopher Bigsby, Cambridge 1997, S. 60–85.

– (Hrsg.) *Approaches to Teaching Miller's* »*Death of a Salesman*«, New York 1995.

Schockley, John S., »*Death of a Salesman* and American Leadership: Life Imitates Art«, in: *Journal of American Culture* 17.2 (Summer 1994) S. 49–56.

Siebold, Thomas (Hrsg.), *Readings on* »*Death of a Salesman*«, San Diego 1999.

– (Hrsg.) *Readings on Arthur Miller*, San Diego 1997.

Stavney, Anne, »Reverence and Repugnance: Willy Loman's Sentiments Toward His Son Biff«, in: *Journal of American Drama and Theatre* 4.2 (Spring 1992) S. 54–62.

Steyn, Mark, »The Revenge of Art«, in: *The New Criterion* 17.7 (1999) S. 46–50.

Tyson, Lois, »The Psychological Politics of the American Dream: *Death of a Salesman* and the Case for an Existential Dialectics«, in: *Essays in Literature* 19.2 (Fall 1992) S. 260–278.

Witt, Jonathan, »Song of the Unsung Antihero: How Arthur Miller's *Death of a Salesman* Flatters Us«, in: *Literature and Theology* 12.2 (1998) S. 205–216.

Nachwort

I

Arthur Miller gilt der Literaturkritik seit den Anfängen seiner Karriere als einer der gesellschaftskritisch und politisch engagiertesten Autoren unter den neueren amerikanischen Dramatikern. Seine Biographie, sein bisheriges Werk und insbesondere sein erfolgreichstes Drama, *Death of a Salesman*, werden gern als Beleg für diese Einordnung herangezogen. Miller ist sich der Etikettierung früh bewußt geworden, und er hat sich dagegen zur Wehr gesetzt. So schreibt er etwa mit einem Seitenblick auf sein populärstes Werk in einem seiner Kommentare:

> »A muffled debate arose with the success of *Death of a Salesman* in which attempts were made to justify or dismiss the play as a Left-wing piece or as a Right-wing manifestation of decadence. The presumption underlying both views is that a work of art is the sum of its author's political outlook, real or alleged, and more, that its political implications are valid elements in its aesthetic evaluation. I do not believe this either for my own or for other writers' works.«

Trotz dieser expliziten Warnung kann man aber nicht umhin, zum einen die gesellschaftskritische Dimension in Millers Werk zu betonen und zum anderen die Verbindungslinien zwischen der kritischen Haltung und der Lebenserfahrung dieses Autors zur Kenntnis zu nehmen.

Schon die frühen Jahre Millers waren geprägt von problematischen Erfahrungen, die die Erlebnisse der Wirtschaftskatastrophe von 1929, schwierige Familienverhältnisse und einen bald einsetzenden Kampf um den sozialen Aufstieg einschlossen. Miller wurde am 17. Oktober 1915 als Sohn eines kleinen Textilfabrikanten in New York City geboren. Sein Vater geriet schon im Vorfeld der »Great Depression« in finanzielle Schwierigkeiten, und die Familie zog 1929 nach Brooklyn um, wo Miller die James Madison und die Abraham Lincoln High Schools besuchte. Er war während dieser Zeit ein recht durch-

schnittlicher Schüler, der mehr Wert auf Sport als auf irgend-
welche intellektuellen Betätigungen legte. Als er 1932 die High
School mit einem wenig spektakulären Abschluß verließ, stand
er vor dem Dilemma, daß weder die finanziellen Verhältnisse
der Familie noch seine mageren Abschlußnoten einen pro-
blemlosen Übergang auf das College erlaubten. So schlug sich
Miller, nachdem er von der University of Michigan als Student
abgelehnt worden war, zunächst einmal für etwa zweieinhalb
Jahre als phantasievoller Gelegenheitsarbeiter durch. Die
»odd jobs«, die er während dieser Zeit der Suche übernahm,
umfaßten Beschäftigungen als Lastwagenfahrer, Fabrikarbei-
ter, Kellner, Angestellter in einer Firma für Autozubehör und
als Sänger bei einer regionalen Radiostation. Es waren die
Erfahrungen dieser Jahre seines Lebens, die zweierlei bei
Miller bewirkten. Zum einen brachten sie ihn in Kontakt mit
Sozialschichten, die im besonderen Maße unter den wirtschaft-
lichen Schwierigkeiten der Zeit litten; und zum anderen weck-
ten sie sein Bestreben, durch Selbstdisziplin und harte Arbeit
der Misere zu entrinnen und eine Karriere anzustreben, die
seinem Ehrgeiz und seinen Talenten entsprach.

Eine Chance dazu bot sich im Jahre 1934, als die University of
Michigan ihn bei einer erneuten Bewerbung trotz seiner mäßi-
gen Noten zum Studium zuließ, das er mit Ersparnissen der
früheren Jahre sowie durch weitere Gelegenheitsarbeit finan-
zierte. Miller studierte zunächst Journalistik, gewann schnell
Anschluß an Kreise, in denen die sozialen und politischen
Probleme der Zeit diskutiert wurden, und wandte sich schließlich dem Dramenschreiben zu. Erste Erfolge stellten sich bald
ein: Der junge Autor gewann den Hopwood Preis der Universität für seine Stücke *Honors at Dawn* (1936) und *No Villain*
(1938; später umgearbeitet zu *They Too Arise* und *The Grass
Still Grows*). Schon diese ersten Dramen zeigen Miller als
engagierten Gesellschaftskritiker, der in der Tradition des
zeitgenössischen politischen Theaters soziale Mißstände
anprangert und an das soziale Verantwortungsgefühl seiner
Mitbürger appelliert. Der Erfolg setzte sich fort, als Miller
1938 der Theatre Guild Award verliehen wurde. Im selben

Jahr schloß er sein Universitätsstudium erfolgreich ab, kehrte
nach New York zurück und arbeitete für kurze Zeit im Federal
Theatre Project mit, das als Sammelbecken für die politische
Linke unter den jungen Dramatikern galt. Doch das Ende
solcher politisch motivierten und staatlich finanzierten Pro-
jekte war bald gekommen, und für Miller bedeutete dies den
Anfang einer zweiten ungesicherten Übergangsphase in seiner
Karriere. Immerhin aber war er jetzt schon in der Lage, einen
Teil seines Einkommens durch schriftstellerische Auftragsar-
beit (hauptsächlich Hörspiele für die Radioprogramme der
CBS und NBC) zu bestreiten.

Im Jahre 1944 besuchte Miller, der 1940 Mary Grace Slattery
geheiratet hatte, verschiedene Armee-Camps, um Material für
den Film *The Story of GI Joe* zu sammeln. Aus dieser Zeit
stammt auch sein Kriegstagebuch *Situation Normal* (1944).
Ebenfalls 1944 wird Millers erstes Broadway-Stück, *The Man
Who Had All the Luck*, aufgeführt. Das Stück, das sich,
obwohl mit dem Theatre Guild Award ausgezeichnet, als
Versager erweist (nur vier Aufführungen), behandelt ein cha-
rakteristisches Miller-Thema: die Auseinandersetzung zweier
Brüder um die Achtung und Zuneigung ihres Vaters. Im Jahre
1945 folgt die Veröffentlichung des schon erfolgreicheren
Romans *Focus*, der die Problematik des Anti-Semitismus am
Beispiel seines jüdisch aussehenden Protagonisten Lawrence
Newman aufgreift.

Millers erster großer Erfolg, der ihn in die Reihe der beachte-
ten zeitgenössischen Dramatiker aufrücken ließ, stellt sich
1947 mit der Aufführung von *All My Sons* ein. Das Stück, das
thematisch wie stilistisch Ibsen verpflichtet ist, gewinnt 1947
den New York Drama Critics' Circle Award. Es zeichnet eine
Reihe von Themen und Techniken vor, die für den späteren
Miller typisch bleiben sollten. So etwa widmet es sich der
analytischen Darstellung einer sorgsam verdrängten Vergangenheit, in der sich persönliche Schuld, wohlmeinender Op-
portunismus und moralisches Versagen als Antriebskräfte ent-
hüllen, die eine ganze Familie in die Katastrophe treiben.
Neben den Motiven der problematischen Vergangenheitsbe-

wältigung, der »Lebenslüge«, des Vater-Sohn-Konfliktes und
der Familienproblematik umschreibt das Stück dabei insbesondere den Gedanken, daß der einzelne sich nie der Verantwortung für die anderen, ja für das kommunale Ganze zu entzie-
hen vermag. Im Hinblick auf diese zentrale Einsicht ist es auch
zutreffend, wenn die Kritik *All My Sons* eine Schlüsselrolle in
der Entwicklung Millers zugeschrieben hat. Denn wenn sich
der Autor vorher primär auf eine propagandistisch eingefärbte
und eher allgemein wirkende Kapitalismuskritik zu konzentrieren schien, so findet er jetzt zur dramatischen Gestaltung
gesellschaftlicher und politischer Konflikte, wie sie das Leben
des einzelnen konkret und unabweisbar bestimmen.

Der Erfolg von *All My Sons* wird von der Resonanz auf *Death
of a Salesman* (1949), das neben dem Pulitzer-Preis zahlreiche
andere Auszeichnungen erhält, noch weit übertroffen. Von
jetzt an zählt Miller unbestritten zu den führenden amerikanischen Dramatikern seiner Zeit. 1950 legt er eine Adaption von
Ibsens *An Enemy of the People* vor. Im Jahre 1953 folgt – nach
der erfolgreichen Verfilmung von *Death of a Salesman* – das
Drama *The Crucible*, das auf mancherlei Weise eine herausge-
hobene Stellung im Miller-Kanon einnimmt. Zum einen greift
es nämlich mit der Darstellung der Salemer Hexenprozesse
gegen Ende des 17. Jahrhunderts historische Ereignisse auf,
die das Gewissen der Nation noch immer belasten. Zum
anderen bieten sich als Analogie zur Massenhysterie im purita-
nischen Salem der Vergangenheit umstrittene politische Vor-
gänge der Gegenwart an, nämlich die anti-kommunistischen
»witch-hunts« der fünfziger Jahre, bei denen sich insbesondere
Senator Joseph McCarthy hervortat. Und schließlich wirkt das
Stück aus späterer Sicht wie eine prophetische Vorwegnahme
der Auseinandersetzung um Millers eigene politische Schwierigkeiten, die er bald mit dem berüchtigten House Committee
on Un-American Activities haben sollte. *The Crucible* wird
von der amerikanischen Öffentlichkeit zunächst nur halbherzig
zur Kenntnis genommen. Doch die Popularität des Stückes in
Europa weckt die Aufmerksamkeit und führt außerdem zu
politischen Kontroversen. So wird Miller 1954, als er der

belgischen Uraufführung in Brüssel beiwohnen will, von den Behörden die Ausstellung eines Reisepasses verweigert.

Im folgenden Jahr bringt Miller zwei Einakter heraus. *A Memory of Two Mondays* (1955) lebt von Millers Rückerinnerung an seine eigenen Erfahrungen als kleiner Angestellter in einem »auto supply shop«. *A View from the Bridge* (1955; ein Jahr später in erweiterter Fassung in London aufgeführt) präsentiert eine Art moderne Tragödie im Milieu der italienischen Einwandererkolonie von Brooklyn.

Die Zeit um 1955/56 markiert den Anfang einer längeren Periode persönlicher und politischer Schwierigkeiten in Millers Leben. Er läßt sich zunächst von seiner ersten Frau scheiden und wird bald darauf immer stärker in die Konflikte zwischen politisch links stehenden Intellektuellen und übereifrigen Untersuchungsbehörden, die überall kommunistische Unterwanderung wittern, hineingezogen. Miller wird 1956 vor das Committee on Un-American Activities zitiert, und es zeigt sich, daß er entschlossen ist, politische Position zu beziehen. Er bekennt sich zu seinen sozialistischen Ideen und Sympathien der Vergangenheit, leugnet aber, jemals Mitglied der kommunistischen Partei gewesen zu sein, und weigert sich zudem, andere Personen zu benennen, die an bestimmten von der kommunistischen Partei unterstützten Schriftstellertreffen des Jahres 1947 teilgenommen hatten. Miller verhält sich damit ähnlich wie sein Protagonist John Proctor in *The Crucible*, der am Ende des Stückes die persönliche Stigmatisierung zwar nicht scheut, aber keineswegs gewillt ist, darüber hinaus zum Auslöser für den Niedergang anderer zu werden. Millers unbeugsame Haltung bringt ihm eine Verurteilung wegen »contempt of congress« ein, die allerdings später von einem Appellationsgericht aufgrund einer vordergründigen legalistischen Argumentation wieder zurückgezogen wird.

Doch nicht nur politische Konflikte bestimmten das Leben des Autors um diese Zeit. Er heiratet 1956 die Schauspielerin Marilyn Monroe, und die Presse wittert in der Prominentenehe sofort eine Quelle für mögliche Sensationsberichte. In der Tat scheint Miller in der Folgezeit Probleme zu haben, die seiner

Schriftstellerei abträglich sind. Er schreibt zunächst keine neuen Dramen mehr und bringt es bis 1964 nur zu einem Drehbuch für den Film *The Misfits* (1960/61), das auf eine stark modifizierte frühere Kurzgeschichte zurückgeht. Erst 1964 – Miller war inzwischen von Marilyn Monroe geschieden worden – tritt er mit *After the Fall* wieder als Dramatiker an die Öffentlichkeit. Doch das Stück zeigt noch deutlich die Spuren der politischen wie persönlichen Probleme der letzten Jahre. Sowohl das Verhältnis des Protagonisten Quentin zu seiner attraktiven, aber hochneurotischen Frau Maggie als auch seine Verstrickungen in anti-kommunistische Säuberungswellen geben der Kritik Anlaß, die wenig überzeugend umgesetzten autobiographischen Elemente des Dramas zu bemängeln.

Dennoch markiert die Mitte der sechziger Jahre den Beginn einer neuen Phase im Schaffen Arthur Millers. Nach seiner Eheschließung mit der Photographin Ingeborg Morath im Jahre 1962 bringt er außer *After the Fall* in schneller Folge *Incident at Vichy* (1964), die Kurzgeschichtensammlung *I Don't Need You Any More* (1967) und das Drama *The Price* (1968) heraus. *Incident at Vichy* befaßt sich mit der Nazi-Verfolgung mißliebiger Personen im besetzten Frankreich und betont eindringlich die Problematik persönlicher Verantwortung in sozialen Ausnahmesituationen. *The Price* kehrt zu den Themen der Vergangenheitsbewältigung, des Bruder-Konfliktes und zum Motiv der Außenseiterexistenz zurück. Die Anerkennung Millers als bedeutender und politisch bewußt agierender Gegenwartsautor schlägt sich in den sechziger Jahren auch in seiner Wahl zum Präsidenten (1965) der Schriftstellervereinigung P. E. N. nieder.

In den siebziger Jahren versucht sich Miller in *The Creation of the World and Other Business* (1972) an der Komödie, wobei er eine komische Version der Genesis-Geschichte zum Zentrum seines Dramas macht. Das Stück fällt wenig überzeugend aus, und Miller antwortet trotzig auf die zum Teil beißende Kritik, indem er ein Musical, *Up from Paradise* (1974), daraus macht. Es folgen 1977 *The Archbishop's Ceiling*, eine Auseinandersetzung mit dem Schicksal von Schriftsteller-Dissidenten unter kommunistischem Regime, und im Frühjahr 1980 *The Ameri-can Clock*, eine Adaption von Studs Terkels Dokumentation *Hard Times*, die sich mit den Folgen der »Great Depression« für das amerikanische Alltagsleben, insbesondere aber den Zusammenhalt der Familie befaßt. Dem Thema der Judenver-folgung am Beispiel von Auschwitz wendet sich Miller 1980 in *Playing for Time* zu, einem Fernsehstück, für das er das Drehbuch schreibt. In der Zwischenzeit waren unter dem Titel *The Theater Essays of Arthur Miller* (1978) auch seine theoreti-schen Beiträge zu Problemen des Dramas und des Theaters erschienen.

In den letzten Jahren ist es merklich stiller um Arthur Miller geworden. Er lebt zurückgezogen in Connecticut und verlagert seit einiger Zeit seine schriftstellerischen Aktivitäten auch auf ganz andere Gebiete als seine ehemalige dramatische Do-mäne. So etwa hat er zusammen mit Ingeborg Morath die Bild/ Textbände *In Russia* (1969), *In the Country* (1977) und *Chinese Encounters* (1979) herausgebracht, bei denen er für den Text verantwortlich zeichnet.

II

Daß Millers populärstes und bedeutendstes Drama *Death of a Salesman* zugleich auch dasjenige ist, welches die meisten Kommentare herausgefordert hat, kann wohl kaum verwun-dern. Erstaunlicher ist es schon, wie wenig sich Kritiker und Kommentatoren über die Themen und Tendenzen oder über die formale Gestaltung des Stückes einig zu werden vermoch-ten. Zwar ist der Kreis der Probleme, die immer wieder diskutiert werden, ein relativ begrenzter, aber es gibt kaum eine These zu diesem Drama, der von der Kritik nicht unmit-telbar auch eine ganz andere These – bis hin zum diametralen Widerspruch – entgegengesetzt worden wäre. Folglich bietet es sich für eine Skizze kritischer Bestandsaufnahme an, rekur-rente Fragen und Probleme kenntlich zu machen, nicht aber einseitig deren oft umstrittene Lösungen zu referieren.

Ein erstes Problemfeld konstituiert sich durch die Frage nach der Gesellschaftskritik in *Death of a Salesman*. Soll hier das

System der Konkurrenzgesellschaft und des ökonomischen Verdrängungskampfes unter Verweis auf das Beispiel Willy Loman angeklagt werden? Zeigt das Drama die Folgen eines schrankenlosen und inhumanen Kapitalismus auf, in dessen Umfeld der einzelne, insbesondere aber der Schwache, funktionalisiert und seiner selbst entfremdet wird, bis er am Ende als unnütz und verbraucht ausgeschieden werden kann? Geht es Miller um die Kritik an spezifisch amerikanischen Zuständen, oder meint er die moderne westliche Gesellschaft als solche? Wie vergleicht sich Millers Sozialkritik mit den bisweilen zur sozialrevolutionären Propaganda ausufernden Dramen der »red decade«? Wird Willy Loman zum hilflosen Opfer der Gesellschaft oder macht er sich selbst zum Opfer, indem er deren Spielregeln auf naive Weise mißversteht?

Gerade die letztere Frage leitet über auf ein zweites Problemfeld: die kritische Sichtung der von einzelnen Personen oder bestimmten Personengruppen unreflektiert akzeptierten Wertwelt. Das Stück ist immer wieder als radikale Kritik am »American Dream« verstanden worden. Doch umstritten bleibt dabei, welche Form des »American Dream« – ein notorisch vages Konzept – bei Miller gemeint ist. Wird hier eine pervertierte moderne Spielart des amerikanischen Traums dekuvriert, der sich seiner inneren Substanz (so etwa der Ideale von Freiheit, Gleichheit und Menschenwürde) entledigt hat und nur noch auf ihrer entäußerten Form des persönlichen Erfolges beharrt? Oder werden auch historische Vorformen des heutigen Traums kritisiert, indem etwa der Freiheitsdrang und die pastorale Verantwortungslosigkeit von Willys Vater sowie der in anachronistisches Glücksrittertum umschlagende Pioniergeist von Ben keineswegs nur positiv dargestellt werden?

Dergleichen Fragen wiederum leiten über zu einem dritten Problemkomplex, der die Themen: Leitbilder, Familie und das gespannte Vater-Sohn-Verhältnis umfaßt. Als Korrektiv zu Willy Lomans Irrweg bieten sich im Drama verschiedene Person gewordene Lebensmodelle an, die teils aus der Sicht des Protagonisten, teils aus der des Zuschauers geglückter erscheinen mögen. So wählt sich Willy offenkundig seinen Vater, seinen Bruder Ben und den Vertreter Dave Singleman zu Vorbildern, wobei allerdings für den Zuschauer deutlich wird, daß es sich bei den ersteren beiden um problematische Leitbilder handelt, während Singleman ein Modell repräsentiert, das nicht mehr zeitgemäß ist. Und auch Willys Nachbar Charley sowie sein erfolgreicher Sohn Bernard – von einigen Kritikern voreilig als die geglückte Verkörperung amerikanischer Lebensweise hingestellt – fordern zur Kritik heraus (vgl. etwa Charleys zynische Selbstcharakterisierung: »My salvation is that I never took any interest in anything«, S. 102). Problematisch scheint in diesem Zusammenhang bei Miller auch das Bild der Familie zu sein, die sich wechselweise als letzter Zufluchtsort, aber auch als Quelle innerer Spannungen darstellt. Insbesondere das gespannte Vater-Sohn-Verhältnis (Willy und Biff) – ein vertrautes und zentrales Thema in den Dramen Arthur Millers – hat dabei die Kritik zu Interpretationen stimuliert, die bis zur Umdeutung des Stückes als Ödipus-Drama reichen. Aus der umfassenden Perspektive der Familien- und Beziehungsproblematik erscheint es dann plötzlich auch fraglich, wer überhaupt der Protagonist des Stückes ist: Willy Loman, sein Sohn Biff, die amerikanische Familie schlechthin?

Auf einer anderen Ebene der Diskussion liegt die von der Kritik immer wieder betonte Genre-Problematik, die sich in der Debatte niedergeschlagen hat, ob *Death of a Salesman* als moderne Tragödie angesehen werden müsse, ja, ob und wie eine moderne Tragödie überhaupt gedacht werden könne? Die Diskussion bezieht sich in der Regel auf stark divergierende Begriffe des Tragischen, die sich von Aristoteles' *Poetik* über Hegel bis hin zu Millers eigenen Auseinandersetzungen in den Essays »Tragedy and the Common Man«, »The Nature of Tragedy« und »On Social Plays« erstrecken. Immer wieder umkreiste Kernprobleme sind dabei die Fragen nach der menschlichen Statur oder der Würde des Helden, nach der Einsicht in sein Schicksal (die modifizierte »anagnorisis« des Aristoteles) sowie nach der dem »hohen« Gegenstand adäquaten oder nicht adäquaten Sprache des Dramas und seiner auf den Zuschauer abzielenden, »reinigenden« Wirkung. Die Debatte um das Problem der tragischen Einsicht erweist sich dabei als besonders kontrovers und mündet letztlich in die Frage, ob Miller vielleicht bewußt versucht habe, traditionelle Attribute des tragischen Helden – wie etwa seine selbstverschuldete Verblendung und die Einsicht in diese lebenszerstörende Verblendung – auf zwei Personen des Dramas, nämlich Willy Loman und Biff, zu verteilen?

Auch die formalen Besonderheiten von *Death of a Salesman* haben eine Diskussion ausgelöst, die keineswegs auf den Fluchtpunkt einheitlicher Antworten zustrebt. Die auffallende Verwendung von Symbolen, die Effekte der Licht- und Musikregie, die komplexe Überlagerung verschiedener Zeitebenen, der Perspektivenwechsel zwischen realistischer Gegenwartshandlung und imaginären Vergangenheitsereignissen sowie das ebenso einfache wie multifunktionale Bühnenbild, das die Vorstellungskraft des Zuschauers herausfordert, haben zu der Auseinandersetzung geführt, ob das Stück eher in der Tradition des realistisch-naturalistischen Theaters oder aber überwiegend als expressionistisches Drama zu sehen sei. Doch hier wie auch in bezug auf andere Fragen kann die Antwort wohl nur aus einem differenzierten »sowohl als auch« bestehen: Miller versteht es eben, die realistischen und naturalistischen Elemente des Stückes so mit expressionistischen Darstellungstechniken zu verschmelzen, daß eine neue, durchaus eigenständige Einheit entsteht.

Die Liste der kurz skizzierten Themenkomplexe ist damit keineswegs erschöpft. Andere Aspekte, die in bezug auf *Death of a Salesman* immer wieder erwähnt werden, schließen die Frage nach der Selbstfindung und nach dem Funktionieren der Kommunikation innerhalb des Dramas ein; oder sie lenken unsere Aufmerksamkeit auf das Wechselspiel zwischen Wirklichkeitserfassung und imaginärer Rückerinnerung (der Arbeitstitel des Stückes lautete ursprünglich *The Inside of His Head*); oder aber sie führen zu dem umfassenden Problem, ob Willy Loman eher als prototypischer moderner Jedermann

oder doch nur als zeittypische Erscheinung spezifisch amerikanischer Sozialentwicklungen zu sehen sei.

Wie auch immer: Nimmt man die Themenvielfalt von *Death of
a Salesman* mit den dramaturgischen Besonderheiten des
Stücks zusammen und bedenkt zugleich, daß auf beiden
Gebieten die offenen Fragen die abschließenden Antworten
überwiegen, so zeigt sich Millers Drama als ein komplexes
Gebilde, dessen Reiz nicht zuletzt in gewissen Ambiguitäten
und in der notwendig unabschließbaren Auseinandersetzung
mit diesen Ambiguitäten liegt. Es ist schon so, wie Gerald
Weales in der Einleitung zu seiner informativen Textausgabe
und Anthologie kritischer Aufsätze zu diesem Stück sagt: »The
play that can be pinned down, labeled accurately, seen clearly
from one view is a dead one, and *Salesman* is certainly not
that.«

Bamberg, November 1983   *Manfred Pütz*

Inhalt

Fremdsprachentexte

IN RECLAMS UNIVERSAL-BIBLIOTHEK

Amerikanische Literatur

Philipp Reclam jun. Stuttgart